The Object Lessons [...] to magic: the books [...] and animate them w[...] political struggle, science, and popular mythology. Filled with fascinating details and conveyed in sharp, accessible prose, the books make the everyday world come to life. Be warned: once you've read a few of these, you'll start walking around your house, picking up random objects, and musing aloud: 'I wonder what the story is behind this thing?'"

Steven Johnson, author of *Where Good Ideas Come From* and *How We Got to Now*

Object Lessons describes themselves as 'short, beautiful books,' and to that, I'll say, amen. . . . If you read enough Object Lessons books, you'll fill your head with plenty of trivia to amaze and annoy your friends and loved ones—caution recommended on pontificating on the objects surrounding you. More importantly, though . . . they inspire us to take a second look at parts of the everyday that we've taken for granted. These are not so much lessons about the objects themselves, but opportunities for self-reflection and storytelling. They remind us that we are surrounded by a wondrous world, as long as we care to look."

John Warner, *The Chicago Tribune*

"The joy of the series, of reading *Remote Control, Golf Ball, Driver's License, Drone, Silence, Glass, Refrigerator, Hotel,* and *Waste* . . . in quick succession, lies in encountering the various turns through which each of their authors has been put by his or her object . . . The object predominates, sits squarely center stage, directs the action. The object decides the genre, the chronology, and the limits of the study. Accordingly, the author has to take her cue from the *thing* she chose or that chose her. The result is a wonderfully uneven series of books, each one a *thing* unto itself."

Julian Yates, *Los Angeles Review of Books*

"The Object Lessons series has a beautifully simple premise. Each book or essay centers on a specific object. This can be mundane or unexpected, humorous or politically timely. Whatever the subject, these descriptions reveal the rich worlds hidden under the surface of things."

Christine Ro, *Book Riot*

". . . a sensibility somewhere between Roland Barthes and Wes Anderson."

Simon Reynolds, author of *Retromania: Pop Culture's Addiction to Its Own Past*

OBJECTLESSONS

A book series about the hidden lives of ordinary things.

Series Editors:

Ian Bogost and Christopher Schaberg

In association with

BOOKS IN THE SERIES

pregnancy test

KAREN WEINGARTEN

BLOOMSBURY ACADEMIC
NEW YORK • LONDON • OXFORD • NEW DELHI • SYDNEY

BLOOMSBURY ACADEMIC
Bloomsbury Publishing Inc
1385 Broadway, New York, NY 10018, USA
50 Bedford Square, London, WC1B 3DP, UK
29 Earlsfort Terrace, Dublin 2, Ireland

BLOOMSBURY, BLOOMSBURY ACADEMIC and the Diana logo are trademarks of
Bloomsbury Publishing Plc

First published in the United States of America 2023

Copyright © Karen Weingarten, 2023

Cover design: Alice Marwick

For legal purposes the Acknowledgements on p. 131 constitute an extension
of this copyright page.

A catalog record for this book is available from the Library of Congress.

ISBN: PB: 978-1-5013-7654-2
ePDF: 978-1-5013-7656-6
eBook: 978-1-5013-7655-9

Series: Object Lessons

Typeset by Deanta Global Publishing Services, Chennai, India
Printed and bound in the United States of America

To find out more about our authors and books visit www.bloomsbury.com and
sign up for our newsletters.

For Shelly, my sister

CONTENTS

INTRODUCTION

The first time I took a pregnancy test it was positive. There are parts of the experience I still remember: the Rite Aid I visited on my way home from a poetry reading. The bright lights of the drugstore and the dread—and self-consciousness—in my body as I waited to pay for the test. I don't remember which test I chose, but it must have been the cheapest, perhaps the generic Rite Aid brand, because I was a broke graduate student at the time. And then I remember skimming the instructions before peeing awkwardly on the stick while wondering whether I was doing it correctly. I also remember that second line appearing almost instantly while I held the test against the black-and-white-checkered bathroom floor in the rented apartment I shared with my roommate. The next day I took a bus to the Planned Parenthood in Brooklyn.

"Can a positive pregnancy test ever be wrong?" I asked the receptionist at the front desk when I arrived. "Nope," she responded. "Take a seat." And I joined a full waiting room to confirm results I knew then were likely accurate. I also knew I was going to have an abortion, but I thought that first a doctor would give me another, perhaps more accurate, pregnancy test. But no, my own report of a positive home pregnancy test was enough to convince them that I was, in fact, pregnant. Instead, I was given a sonogram and learned I was six weeks along.

Since then I've taken many pregnancy tests, but it wasn't until my sister had a chemical pregnancy that I stopped to think about the history of this small object that has played such a significant part in my life. Chemical pregnancies happen when an egg has been fertilized and starts the process of implantation but then doesn't take, and they're far more common than most people realize. Most people don't know when they've had a chemical pregnancy because the process barely disrupts a normal menstrual cycle. If you're hoping to be pregnant, however, and regularly testing for pregnancy, then you might register a chemical pregnancy, as my sister did. When my sister saw a barely-there second line, days before her period was expected, which vanished a few days later when she took another test, I started questioning the science behind the pregnancy test. I discovered that before home pregnancy tests were so accessible, women would have never known a chemical pregnancy had occurred and never experienced the pregnancy as a loss. The ephemeral nature of chemical pregnancies made me wonder whether it was even accurate to call them pregnancies at all. Were they only considered pregnancies because the pregnancy test could detect them? This question led me to another: What is the pregnancy test even testing?

These questions unlocked the history of pregnancy diagnosis for me, which transformed how I now see the commonplace pregnancy test wand. A lot has been written about the pregnancy test in various online platforms, newspapers, and magazines, but because the history is sometimes convoluted—with competing interests involving corporations and scientists and doctors—it's not always easy to untangle how exactly the home pregnancy test became such an integral object in our reproductive lives. This book aims to acknowledge this complicated history but also address how the pregnancy test has not always lived up to the promise that more information about our bodies is enlightening or liberating. While science so often promises clear-cut answers, the reality of pregnancy—and pregnancy testing—is much messier. In some cases, the scientists working in reproductive endocrinology (the study of reproductive hormones) or in immunology (the study of immune systems and antibodies), two fields that led to the pregnancy test we know today, didn't have the development of a pregnancy test in mind when they were discovering ways to isolate hormones or measure them. Just as there are many people who could be credited with playing a role in the pregnancy test's invention, there were also many prototypes along the way and many people who influenced each other. The pregnancy test we have today is exemplary of how most scientific discoveries come about: not through a single eureka moment but through incremental collaborative innovations.

While no person is solely responsible for inventing pregnancy testing, the most important role in the story is undoubtedly played by the hormone human chorionic gonadotropin, or hCG. Whether it's mentioned or not, hCG's influence is present on every page of this book because it's what all accurate pregnancy tests have relied on: detecting whether or not hCG is there. Recognizing this hormone's existence was crucial to the first pregnancy test invented in 1927, but because the first scientists that identified it as critical to pregnancy understood so little about it—thinking it was produced by the pituitary gland at the bottom of the human brain—they named it "prolan" (from the Latin word for offspring). It took a young doctor-scientist, Georgeanna Seegar Jones, to correctly identify that the placenta makes hCG during pregnancy. She gave the hormone its current name on March 15, 1945 at a talk she presented to the American Physiological Society.[1] Since then, its role in diagnosing pregnancy, infertility, and other reproductive issues has only become more important. Without an understanding of hCG, we wouldn't have today's pregnancy tests.

Within a few years of the invention of the first pregnancy test in 1927, doctors and medical clinics began offering pregnancy testing as a service. These early tests, however, could only be done in a lab because they involved live animals. It wasn't until the late 1960s that the first home pregnancy test was designed, and it took until the late 1970s for it to be marketed in the US. This initial home pregnancy test looked nothing like the tests we use today. The idea of home testing seemed radical to some because it required women to perform basic laboratory work in their bathrooms or kitchens, putting into women's hands a technology that had previously only been available to doctors and lab technicians. Because the invention of the home pregnancy test marked a turning point in the history of our reproductive lives, this book begins with its invention in 1969 before turning to the history that led to its creation.

Although the home pregnancy test was available in Canada and Europe in the early 1970s, laboratory pregnancy tests dominated the American market from the 1930s until the mid-1980s in the United States. These tests, which could only be ordered by a doctor and done in a lab, created a paternalistic medical culture that told women that doctors had more knowledge about their reproductive bodies than they themselves had. And sometimes access to this knowledge was intentionally withheld if a doctor believed a woman might use it to get an abortion or simply because he didn't believe she needed a test. In many ways, the home pregnancy test gave back to women what should have always been theirs: first-hand knowledge about how their bodies worked without the mediation of the medical establishment. At the same time, because reliable pregnancy tests document information about bodies that the human eye might not be able to see, the pregnancy test has at times been used coercively when in the hands of people and institutions invested in controlling pregnant bodies.

The first part of this book covers this history of the pregnancy test in the United States, from the questionable tests of the nineteenth century (and before) to the laboratory pregnancy tests of the 1930s to the home pregnancy test today. Most of this book focuses on the US because the history and cultural reception of pregnancy tests look quite different across the globe. I discuss Canada's important role as the first country to market a home pregnancy test, and the UK's significance as the place where the first stick-shaped test was invented. In the US, there was a reluctance to allow the availability of home pregnancy test in drugstores for over-the-counter purchase, and even after its acceptance, access to the test was uneven along economic and racial lines. The American history of the pregnancy test, not surprisingly, mirrors American history. It's impossible to tell the American history of the home pregnancy test without engaging its racist and classist (and of course, sexist) dimensions. The second half of this book examines how the pregnancy test has been represented in popular culture, and how, in turn, representations of the pregnancy test have influenced our conception of pregnancy. I show how the cultural importance of the home pregnancy test is much bigger than its small size and commonality might suggest at first glance. While the twenty-first-century home pregnancy test has become a familiar object, it started out as an idea about reproductive autonomy and privacy, and its implications have had a greater impact on our reproductive lives than anyone could have imagined.

PART ONE

HISTORY

1 DESIGNING THE HOME PREGNANCY TEST

In the late 1950s, Margaret Crane moved to New York City to attend Parsons Art School with the intention of becoming a fashion illustrator.[1] But as the industry moved away from drawings to photographed models, Crane was advised to become a graphic designer instead. After graduation, she mostly freelanced, temped, and worked at various part-time jobs in the city. In 1967, she accepted a freelancing position for Organon Pharmaceuticals, which at the time was based in West Orange, New Jersey. Even though the commute was long, she hoped it would give her an opportunity to do design work for a new line of cosmetics Organon was developing. She lived in a sixth floor walk-up tenement apartment with two roommates in the Yorkville neighborhood of Manhattan, which meant waking up at dawn to get to West Orange. Her commute involved a bus, the PATH train, and then two more buses, until she eventually reached the single-family house that Organon gave her as an office. She worked in the living room, and the only other employee within earshot was a secretary who worked in the dining room and made clear to Crane from her first day that she wasn't Crane's secretary. In the basement of the house was a large collection of rabbits, which Organon used to test and make their various products. Crane could occasionally hear their screeching from her makeshift office. The clear garbage bags of dead rabbits that regularly appeared outside ensured that the house next door was vacant for a long time.

Although Crane was under the impression that Organon hired her to design and draw products and their packages, from face creams to lipsticks, she found herself mostly doing busy work, like overseeing stock and making sure shipments were mailed correctly. It wasn't work she enjoyed or excelled in. Occasionally, she also helped with advertisements for various cosmetic products, which is why she was asked to visit the lab the day they were working on a stabilization test for a new lotion. As she walked in that morning, she saw ten test tubes hanging over a highly polished angled metal rack, so shiny it looked like a mirror. The sides of each transparent tube were covered in numerical codes, but their clear bottoms were reflected on the gleaming rack. She had befriended an older doctor who worked in the lab, and as she passed by his office she asked him about these mysterious tubes. Pregnancy tests, he responded. Doctors sent Organon urine from women who had come into their office for a pregnancy test. Their clinics shipped Organon the urine in bottles made by the company, and next Organon, using their careful identification system, added the urine to the test tubes with antibodies made for the pregnancy test. They then called back the doctors informing them if the test was negative or positive. While it took two hours to process each test, women usually had to wait several weeks before learning the results. Crane's friend carefully explained how the test worked, and it didn't seem that complicated. She immediately thought, *Why can't women do this themselves?*

This was the late 1960s, a revolutionary time in Crane's own words. As she told me over iced tea in her cozy midtown Manhattan apartment, in the early 1960s she had accompanied a friend who needed an illegal abortion, and she was an early adopter of the birth control pill. Doctors weren't supposed to give unmarried women like Crane prescriptions for the pill, but a friend recommended a sympathetic doctor who overlooked this restriction and wrote her a prescription to help regulate her heavy and painful periods. Slowly, people within and outside the medical establishment became more willing to challenge attitudes toward sex outside of marriage, contraception, sexuality, and masturbation. Why couldn't women also take a pregnancy test without the watchful eye of a patronizing doctor?

The evening after Crane first spotted the laboratory pregnancy tests, during her long commute home, she thought about how the neat row of test tubes could be converted into a product women could use at home. Finding ways to design products using simple and clean lines was something she loved doing. She had a second job in the evenings at a print shop on Houston Street, and there she started digging around for some materials to design a prototype for a home pregnancy test. Her first design was made out of cardboard and roughly sketched. She didn't settle on the apparatus for the design until a few days later when her eye landed on a rectangular clear plastic container filled with paperclips on her desk. It had a lid that fit securely. She dumped out the paper clips, made a plastic shelf inside the box with two holes that fit a test tube and eyedropper, and out of a piece of shiny Mylar she made an angled mirror that would reflect the bottom of the test tube to show the results. On New Year's Eve 1967, she stayed late at work to finish her design. Using everyday materials, she had created the prototype for the first home pregnancy test.[2]

Crane's Design

In 1960, seven years before Crane started working on her design, two Swedish doctors invented the laboratory pregnancy test. Crane's invention intended to bring this science into women's hands. It meant packaging the test—which included a small amount of hormones—for at-home use, but Crane was certain that with a good design this was possible.

When she told her boss, the vice president of the company, about her idea he scoffed. First of all, why would Organon

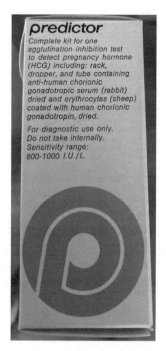

FIGURE 1 The packaging design first created by Meg Crane for Predictor home pregnancy test. Image by author, box courtesy of Meg Crane.

invent a device that would compete with their profitable laboratory pregnancy tests? Organon both manufactured these tests and processed the results for doctors' offices. It was a good business. Second, he added, there was no chance women could manage the many-stepped process to accurately administer the test. It would be a disaster. Her idea was dismissed, and she assumed that would be the end of that chapter.

A few months later, on a cold wintery day that started off terribly, Crane's fate would change in two significant ways, as she vividly remembers. On her way to work, she slipped and landed straight on her bottom. The ground was wet and slushy, and a big wet circle formed on the back of her homemade dress. She might have considered turning back, but she was a freelance worker and needed this job to pay her rent.

Here, she paused when telling me the story: "I still have the pattern for that dress." She kept it to remember that day, but not because she would make history with her pregnancy test design. Rather, it was the day she met the man who would be her partner for the next forty-one years. But that morning she had no idea the meeting would happen when she arrived at work, her dress still uncomfortably wet. The secretary in the next room greeted her by saying, "I heard there's a big meeting today about the design for a home pregnancy test Organon wants to make." Crane hadn't been told. In fact, she had no idea the company had even been discussing a home pregnancy test because her boss had ridiculed her proposal. She immediately went looking for the company's product manager, and he confirmed that the meeting was indeed happening. Fortunately, she had kept a copy of her prototype on her desk. She arrived at the boardroom before the meeting even started, found a seat as close to the radiator as possible, hoping her dress would dry in time, and placed her prototype in front of her on the table.

Slowly, the room filled with twelve men, all in suits, all there to discuss the future of the home pregnancy test. Crane was the only woman present. Shortly before the meeting began, a sub-contracted ad man walked in with two account executives. The ad man's good looks and confidence caught Crane's attention. Later she would learn that his name was Ira Sturtevant, and that he was there to write the advertising copy for the future home pregnancy test. By then, the different prototypes were all lined on the table. There was Crane's no-nonsense and efficient design, last in the line because she put it there herself. Another test was encased in a soft oval plastic container, another had a feminine pink tassel dangling from its cap, and yet another was delicately decorated with diamonds around its perimeter. All the tests, except for Crane's, were designed by men. (When telling me this story, she speculates that because companies forbade designers from discussing designs for new products with even their closest family members, these men wouldn't have even been able to consult with their wives about whether their home pregnancy test design might work for them.) As the meeting began, Sturtevant looked over the designs and picked up Crane's, announcing definitively, "This is the only one we can use."

"No, no, that's the one Meg did for talking purposes," the company vice president quickly responded, referring to Crane with the nickname she uses to this day. "These are the real ones up here," he added, pointing to the ones the designers brought in.

"But look," Sturtevant pointed out, "all these other designs are missing an important component: what will women use to collect urine for the test?" A surprised silence filled the room. No one had thought of this question. "A glass from the kitchen cupboard?" someone tentatively suggested, realizing as he spoke that this idea didn't sound savory. Only Crane's design had anticipated this step.

Here is how Crane's home pregnancy test worked: the entire package was small and could easily fit into a woman's hand. Later a newspaper would compare its dimensions to a package of king-sized cigarettes.[3] The container for the test was made of a hard, clear plastic rectangular box, and women were instructed to collect their urine in its square-shaped cap. Then using an eyedropper, they extracted just a few milliliters of urine and added it to the test tube, which was already prepared with dried rabbit antibodies and sheep blood.

Tap water also had to be added. (In later models, small packets of distilled water would be included with the test.) Once the fluids were mixed together, the container had to be left undisturbed for two hours. It was critical that it sit somewhere with no vibrations or movement or the results would be difficult if not impossible to read. If a woman was pregnant, the substance in the bottom of the test tube formed into the shape of a reddish-brown doughnut that would be reflected in the mirror fitted at the bottom of the container.

FIGURE 2 Early Predictor home pregnancy test sold in Canada and Europe. Image courtesy of Meg Crane.

The doughnut could be thick or thin, but if it was there, it was fairly certain that the woman was pregnant. No doughnut meant no pregnancy. Broken red lines suggested that the test should be done again because the results were ambiguous.

This first home pregnancy test was certainly not simple compared to the ones available today. It was a twelve-step process that resembled something like a high school chemistry experiment, but was it any more difficult than following a cake recipe?

Still, there were objections. Organon executives complained that Crane's design used materials that were too expensive for mass production. The plastic container—the most ingenious component of the test because it was transparent, allowed light in so the results could be viewed easily, and stabilized the contraption—was supposedly too costly to manufacture for these purposes. So Crane took three days off work (at no pay since she was an hourly worker) with the mission to find a plastics manufacturer who could make the box at an affordable price. She called and visited plastic companies in the Bronx, Newark, and Long Island, until finally a Pennsylvania company told her they could make the box at a third of the price estimated by the Organon executives. With that last hurdle out of the way, the home pregnancy test was patented with Crane's design. Because corporations can't patent inventions themselves, Crane agreed to sell her rights to the design for $1 in 1969, although she wryly noted to me, "I never did get that $1, nor did they ever send me the paperwork for the patent as

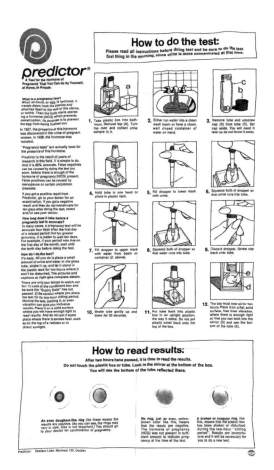

FIGURE 3 Instruction leaflet provided with Predictor home pregnancy test. Copy written by Ira Sturtevant, drawings by Meg Crane. Image by author, leaflet courtesy of Meg Crane.

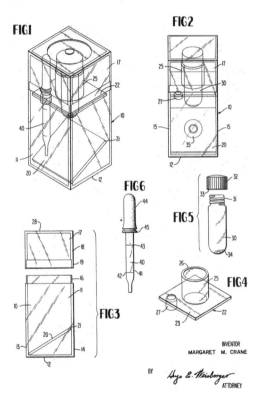

FIGURE 4 Meg Crane's patent for the home pregnancy test design. Filed with US patent office on January 22, 1969. Image courtesy of US patent office.

promised." Besides the salary paid by Organon during the months she worked designing the product and its packaging, she never made a profit off her invention.

However, Sturtevant—that handsome ad man who picked up her design and insisted it was the one—well, she fell in love with him at first sight. When she went home that evening, she told her roommate that she had met the man who would be the love of her life, and after her pregnancy test design was accepted by Organon she had reason to work with him day after day. At the beginning, their meetings were strictly business. They discussed the details of the design for the test, which Organon had named Predictor; Crane interviewed women to ask what color she should use for the swirly P she designed for the test's logo. She wanted both the design and color to be soothing and to have a clean, clinical look, especially for anxious women who might be feeling early symptoms of nausea. After several weeks of working together, one evening, after a day's work, Sturtevant suggested they have a drink together at the Barclay Hotel in midtown Manhattan. A few months later he moved in with her. Soon after that, they opened their own ad agency. Sturtevant was the copy chief; Crane the designer.

Predictor in Canada

While Sturtevant and Crane would remain a couple until Sturtevant's death in 2008, the story of the home pregnancy test in the US didn't have as much immediate success. Organon filed two patents in Crane's name on January 22, 1969, and then started mass production of the home pregnancy test. However, there was staunch opposition in the US. News articles suggested that a home pregnancy test was unreliable, and if available, some women might get a false positive result and rush to get an unnecessary abortion, while others might get a false negative and not seek prompt medical attention.[4] The argument made by medical practitioners, pharmaceutical companies, and the media was that only doctors and laboratories should be able to administer this test and convey such important news. So Organon turned to a more willing market: Canada.

Why Canada? One possible explanation is that Organon saw Canada as a test case for the United States. In 1969, Canada legalized abortion in cases where the pregnancy was deemed to physically or emotionally cause harm to the woman, and in metropolitan areas, many doctors interpreted the new law liberally. A home pregnancy test would give women an easier way to learn whether they were pregnant, and furthermore, women could already take a pregnancy test through pharmacies without a doctor's prescription, which was still illegal to do in the US. Therefore, marketing a home pregnancy test in Canada first could allow Organon to assess the demand for such a product.

There was another side to the story as well: Denver Chemical Manufacturing Co., another pharmaceutical company, was also seriously looking into marketing a home pregnancy test through their Canadian subsidiary, Denver Laboratories. Confidelle, as their product came to be called, was set to be sold in stores by late 1970. While there's little evidence that Organon saw the release of Confidelle as a motivation to offer a competing product, the Canadian pregnancy test's only full-page ad in *Chatelaine*, the most widely circulated Canadian women's magazine, emphasized to readers that its pregnancy test was the first for Canada and the first for the world—and it was Canadian made.

Organon, however, would soon overtake Denver Laboratories with its home pregnancy test. Not only were they willing to take out more advertisements, they could afford to undercut Confidelle and offer their test for a lower price.

Confidelle arrived in Canadian drugstores in early December 1970. (Predictor would follow by summer 1971.) For a suggested price of $5.50 (Canadian dollars), women could discreetly purchase this test and find out at home whether they were pregnant. For comparison, a Maidenform bra, advertised on the same page as an article announcing the test's arrival, cost $6.50.[5] The laboratory test cost $7, presumably because of the number of people involved in its processing. Still, not everyone warmly received the home pregnancy test in Canada.

Just a month after the home pregnancy test's release, *The Province,* a British Columbia newspaper, reported on the test's popularity on the Canadian west coast.[6] Pharmacies regularly sold out of the test, the journalist noted. Yet Bob

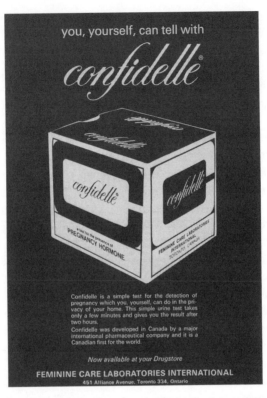

FIGURE 5 Advertisement for Confidelle, the first home pregnancy test marketed in Canada. Published *Chatelaine*, September 1971, p. 64d.

Porte, a local British Columbian pharmacist interviewed for the article, said he wouldn't be selling them in his pharmacy. He told the reporter that he didn't think women could be trusted to accurately obtain results. His pharmacy would only continue offering the (more expensive) laboratory test. Almost a year later, an article in *The Calgary Herald* describes the home pregnancy test as part of a "craze" for other home medical tests, like an at-home Pap Smear (the test was mailed away for results), a "do-it-yourself Child Selection Kit" that promised it could help you choose the sex of your child, and a test called "Pre-Na-Tell" that supposedly predicted the sex of the fetus during pregnancy.[7] The article dismisses these tests, including the home pregnancy test, as passing fads that couldn't be trusted.

Despite these criticisms, the home pregnancy did decently well on the Canadian market, especially in bigger cities, and kept selling, albeit slowly. American women who lived close to the Canadian border often crossed it to procure their own test. One pharmacy in Windsor, Ontario reported that fifty percent of home pregnancy tests were purchased by American women.[8] In Europe and the UK, similar pregnancy tests were also marketed successfully. Still, the hemagglutination inhibition test, as it came to be called because of the science behind it, never achieved the level of popularity of later home pregnancy tests. Doctors often undermined them, insisting they were not as accurate as pregnancy tests in the lab, and it was true that the slightest vibration—a drawer opening and closing underneath or a child running past it—might mess up the results and require a second test.

Time is on Your Side at Last

In the United States, a different narrative unfolded. Even before the home pregnancy test emerged as a reality, laboratory pregnancy tests were far more regulated in the US than in Europe and Canada. By the 1960s, women outside of the US could go to a pharmacy to have a pregnancy test administered by the pharmacist. In the US, however, the pregnancy test was deemed a medical procedure, and only women with a referral from their doctor could take the laboratory test. The results were always processed in a lab, similar to the one Crane visited in Organon. Some feminist and leftist organizations encouraged women to learn how to use the laboratory tests, not marketed for home use, as a way to offer pregnancy tests outside of a doctor's office.[9] In 1973, one small drug store in New Jersey tried to offer the test—the first known American pharmacy that advertised to women that they could process these pregnancy test kits without a doctor's prescription—but eventually, they were shut down and deemed illegal because of a 1953 law that mandated that only people with special licenses could handle bodily fluids.[10] Of course, a physician and laboratory-controlled pregnancy test also ensured that only some women could access it.

Still, the FDA and state health boards weren't always able to keep up with new tests that came on the market. In December 1972, the FDA recalled thousands of home pregnancy tests; as reported by the *New York Times,* the tests were descriptively labeled "do-it-yourself pregnancy detection kits."[11] The tests had been sold and even advertised in women's magazines for a year before the FDA caught on. The agency announced that the tests were being pulled because they were "inaccurate, unreliable and prone to give false results." This version of the home pregnancy test didn't share Crane's design, and its science was more questionable.[12] It was marketed under the name Ova II, and a representative of the company that sold it disputed the FDA's statements, insisting that it was ninety-three percent reliable. Later an independent clinical trial disproved this, showing that Ova II, which supposedly measured the level of estrogen in urine to determine pregnancy, was as accurate as flipping a coin. Ultimately, the FDA didn't take issue with the science underlying the test but argued that it was a drug, and therefore should be subject to the agency's approval before any woman was allowed to use it.[13]

In July 1975, Faraday, Ova II's manufacturer, took the FDA to court and won their case, but not because the judge thought women had a right to test for pregnancy at home.[14] Instead, he argued that it didn't matter whether the test was accurate or not—he believed that "the entire process from conception to delivery or other termination involves observable events and changes in the body that have been known for as long as the human race has propagated itself." In other words, he didn't think a pregnancy test could tell women anything they wouldn't already know soon enough. After all, he explained, anyone taking the test must have had sexual intercourse involving sperm and female genitals and missed at least one menstrual cycle.[15] The pregnancy test, according to his logic, just tested for news that would soon reveal itself without a mediating device and therefore did not constitute a diagnosis.

Despite this ruling, it would take another six years, until 1978, for another home pregnancy test to arrive on the American market. The first reliable American test was branded as e.p.t. (for "early pregnancy test"), and it followed Crane's design for the Predictor models because by then Organon decided it didn't want to be in the over-the-counter business and licensed Crane's design to several pharmaceutical companies.[16] (Within a few months of e.p.t.'s arrival, two more home pregnancy tests would be released using the same design: Answer and Acu-test. Predictor would also soon be introduced to the American market.) The initial print advertisements for e.p.t. were text heavy and often featured smiling heterosexual couples. These ads ended with the note, "Now, when you call your doctor, you have the results of your test to report. Time is on your side at last." This language was meant to reassure an American public that the home pregnancy test wouldn't circumvent the medical establishment, but it remains ambiguous. On the one hand, early pregnancy detection encouraged women to obtain prenatal care as soon as possible, which in the late 1970s was increasingly promoted as women were being told that smoking and drinking alcohol might harm their developing fetus. On the other hand, having time on your side also meant time to contemplate whether you wanted an abortion, especially if you needed to travel to obtain one. By 1978, abortion had been legal in every American state for five years, but that didn't always mean it was accessible. The home pregnancy test gave women time to consider the ramifications of an unplanned pregnancy—and to plan for next steps, including abortion. This consequence of a privately administered pregnancy test couldn't have been far from the minds of the people responsible for this advertisement. This test gave women more options and more time to consider their decisions.

Yet these early home pregnancy tests weren't exactly affordable. The recommended sale price was $10, which was equivalent to about $40 today. Worse, it was recommended that women purchase two tests to confirm the accuracy of the first, especially if it was negative since if the test was taken too early the results could be misleading. The cost of the test therefore limited the market of women who might use it. While there were certainly working-class women, women with limited income of their own, and young women and girls who might have wished to learn whether they were pregnant in the privacy of their homes, the test's high price made it prohibitive for those who didn't have a spare $10 or $20. The home pregnancy test was another reproductive technology only accessible to women with certain means.

After the court ruled in Faraday's favor, the FDA appealed, and more significantly, Congress decided to consider a bill that would give the FDA oversight of medical devices, even if drugs were not involved.[17] Aware of the likelihood that Congress would pass a law classifying the home pregnancy test as a medical device, the American pharmaceutical company Warner-Lambert (later bought by Pfizer) rushed to develop a home pregnancy test before the bill's passage. In the spring of 1976, the company introduced e.p.t. on a small scale.[18] No advertisements were taken out, and the media was nearly silent about the test's introduction. Still, because Warner-Lambert had managed to distribute the test to a limited market before the passage of the 1976 Medical Devices Act, which would ultimately classify home pregnancy tests as a medical device, they did not need to seek official approval for its marketing when it was released more broadly two years later. Shortly after Warner-Lambert released e.p.t., several other pharmaceutical companies followed its example with competing brands; because they all used the same design, they didn't need FDA approval under the 1976 Act.

Why did it take almost eight years after Crane patented the home pregnancy test for it to be marketed in the US? Laboratory pregnancy tests were already big business, and certainly pharmaceutical companies like Organon and medical clinics run by physicians pushed back against a device that would challenge a lucrative system. However, the movement for legal abortion, which was gaining ground in the late 1960s, must have influenced the conversations about whether a home pregnancy test should be introduced to an American market.

In 1967, Colorado passed a law allowing abortion in cases of rape, incest, or if the woman's life was at risk because of the pregnancy. California, North Carolina, and Oregon passed similar laws shortly after. In 1970, Hawaii became the first state to legalize abortion, and that same year New York repealed its anti-abortion laws, opening the door for legal abortions in the first two trimesters. A movement was gaining ground, and before *Roe v. Wade* was decided in 1973 ten more states would follow Hawaii and New York to legalize abortion, either by repealing or passing laws depending on their state's existing statutes. The US was on a threshold in 1970, on the verge of swinging open doors that would allow women to make decisions about their reproductive lives in ways that had been previously foreclosed.

Legal abortion would certainly be an important turning point, but perhaps a home pregnancy test took things a step too far for some people. With a home pregnancy test, women could take control of their decision from day one. They wouldn't need to find a doctor willing to test them for pregnancy who might question their motivations or next steps. They wouldn't need to share their news with anyone until they were ready. The home pregnancy test had the potential to upend a paternalistic culture of gynecological medicine that had worked to convince women that medical doctors knew more about their bodies than they did. It would take eight years before American legislators, pharmaceutical companies, and doctors were willing to accept a home pregnancy test that circumvented their authority—and even then they insisted that each home pregnancy test box, each commercial, and each advertisement include a line urging women to visit their doctor to confirm the results of the test.

Crane never imagined that her freelance job for a giant pharmaceutical company would forever change American women's relationship to pregnancy. Still, she was well aware that in the late 1960s times were changing. "I wasn't a card carrying feminist back then," she told me, "but I did understand that women's lives were constrained because of their gender." Women were pushing back against the social and medical controls that for so long had limited the possibilities of their biological lives. The home pregnancy test made that possible. Time was on our side at last. Or so it seemed.

2 HORMONES

Los Angeles, 1933: in the middle of a deep economic depression the *Los Angeles Times* began advertising pregnancy testing in its classified section, promising women transformative news in just 36 hours. "Bring or mail your urine to the Drug Dept on Figueroa Street" the ad announced, and for only $5 you can know within 36 hours whether you are pregnant.[1] In 1933, $5 would have felt like $100 today, which was a sizable expenditure, but for someone desperate to confirm whether a child was on the way, this might have felt like a reasonable investment.

Within a year, clinics around the city began offering their competing services for commercial pregnancy testing. Sometimes as many as seven ads for the pregnancy test would appear in a single issue of the *Los Angeles Times*, and by 1935 clinics were offering the test for as little as $2, equivalent to $38 today. The language of these ads reflects the motivations and concerns of their potential patients. One 1934 ad lures patients by asking, "Worried over Pregnancy?" Others guarantee accuracy, confidentiality, and even immediacy. "Know within an hour," one ad overpromises. "A refined

FIGURE 6.1 Classified ad for pregnancy test, *Los Angeles Times*, July 22, 1934.

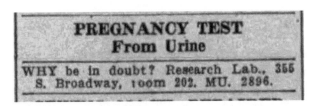

FIGURE 6.2 Classified ad for pregnancy test, *Los Angeles Evening Post Record,* July 18, 1934.

atmosphere," another reassures. The small details in these short ads give only a few hints about what women who paid for these services may have experienced. Several of the ads tell women to bring their morning urine, suggesting that pregnant women in the 1930s were not yet accustomed to the procedure of peeing in a cup in a doctor's office. Other ads promise the services of a licensed doctor, and that results of a positive pregnancy could be detected "after the 7th day," presumably referring to the seventh day after a missed period. The ads' descriptions of clinics as refined and confidential were clearly meant to ease the anxiety of women who felt that using this technology violated the moral codes of femininity, perhaps because their pregnancy was illicit and they hoped to seek an abortion or simply because they sought knowledge that had been previously unavailable to them. Whether the women who sought these services actually found them accurate and trustworthy remains unknown. However, on December 16, 1934 one ad reveals that its clinic offers the "A.Z. pregnancy test," shorthand for the test that in a short number of years became widely known as the most reliable pregnancy test ever invented at that point in history.[2]

The Rabbit Test

The Aschheim-Zondek pregnancy test, often shortened as the A-Z pregnancy test, was named for the two Jewish-German gynecologists, Selmar Aschheim and Bernhard Zondek, who invented it in 1927. It was hailed as the first accurate pregnancy test that used women's urine to determine a positive pregnancy. Like today's pregnancy tests, its error rate was minuscule—less than two percent—if performed correctly, but unlike today's pregnancy tests it had to be administered in a lab because it was messy, complicated, and involved the death of a small animal. Aschheim and Zondek's breakthrough discovery was that pregnant women produce a hormone in their urine—what we now call hCG, the previously mentioned and most important hormone for all pregnancy tests—that is otherwise absent. They were able to isolate the hormone by creating a test that could easily detect hCG in women's urine. That's where the live animals came in.

Aschheim and Zondek turned to white mice, the most commonly used animal in scientific experiments, because they were cheap and easy to obtain. They also found that when young female mice were injected with a pregnant woman's urine in small doses over several days their ovaries swelled significantly in response to hCG. If a woman wasn't pregnant, the mouse's ovaries remained the same. There was an important catch to their test, however, that made it both expensive and controversial: in order to determine whether a woman had hCG in her urine, the mouse's ovaries needed to be examined directly. There was only one known way to do so: the mice had to be killed so that their ovaries could be removed and studied. With every pregnancy test, a mouse died. And thus, the A-Z pregnancy test was complete.[3]

Within a few years after their discovery, Aschheim and Zondek had to flee Germany as Jewish scientists and doctors were removed from their academic posts and not allowed to continue their work. Aschheim moved to Paris and Zondek to Israel, and in those wartime years their research was put on hold. In the meantime, in the United States, Maurice Friedman and Maxwell Lapham at the University of Pennsylvania refined the A-Z test and replaced a mouse with a rabbit. The rabbit's larger size meant she could be injected with urine only once instead of over multiple days like it took with mice. (If too much urine was injected into mice at once, they often died before the procedure was over, leading to questionable results.) The rabbits' ovaries were also bigger, which led to more accurate, easily readable results, although a rabbit still died with every test. The Friedman test, as it became known, was first released in 1931.[4] While doctors recognized the test's potential to transform women's reproductive lives, some were reluctant to embrace it. Keeping and killing animals was expensive and messy, not to mention cruel. And even though women wanted to know whether they were pregnant, and the earlier the better, some doctors and pregnancy guides from the era discouraged women from seeking these tests.[5]

Who would have responded to the ads in the Los Angeles newspapers in the 1930s? The archive is silent on this, but we can imagine: an 18-year old actress who recently moved to Hollywood, hopeful to break into the new and booming industry. She had a casual affair with a director or a screenwriter. Then her period was late, and she worried that it might mean the diaphragm she used had failed or the condom had broken. Maybe she had reason to believe that the Lysol douche she had used, a popular after-sex contraceptive method, also hadn't prevented pregnancy. A pregnancy would have meant the end of her career. In the 1930s, a woman's birth control options were limited; in fact, the term "birth control" itself was only newly invented and the birth control pill was still decades from its realization. The woman clipped the ad from the newspapers and showed it to her lover who gave her the $5 to pay for the test. Or maybe she decided not to say anything and drew on her savings to pay for it. The test gave her knowledge about her body; knowledge that just a few years prior would not have been known to her until the more definitive signs of pregnancy appeared, whether those were the telltale nausea of pregnancy or the fetal kicks that later come with quickening.

Or we can imagine a 38-year old mother with three children who came across the ad for the pregnancy test. Her period was also late, her breasts tender, and she worriedly thought that maybe this was a sign that she was pregnant. Or maybe not, maybe all these symptoms were the hormonal results of getting older and an irregular menstrual cycle. She saved the ad as she contemplated whether to share it with her husband. Neither of them wanted more children, especially in the precarious economy of the Great Depression where financial stability might disappear any day. As one Californian doctor noted in 1933, hardly a day passed that a woman didn't visit his office urgently asking for a pregnancy test. Times were so difficult lately, he sympathetically added, that even women who would have welcomed another baby under different circumstances now headed to an abortionist after receiving positive confirmation of their pregnancy.[6]

In the 1930s abortion was illegal everywhere in the United States, but that didn't mean there weren't options. There were doctors and midwives (some licensed, some not) performing these procedures behind closed doors, sometimes at a great cost—both financially and to a woman's health or life. Women could purchase abortifacients as well, mixtures of herbs that could trigger a miscarriage, if they didn't accidentally die of a poison overdose first. If they had the resources, they could travel overseas or cross the border to Mexico for an abortion, which in the late 1930s was an increasingly popular option as a way to skirt California law.[7] Or, if they turned to the safest option, they could appeal to a board of doctors for a therapeutic abortion, claiming that they must terminate their pregnancies for the sake of their mental or physical health. However, there was no medical consensus among doctors about the reasons that these abortions should be allowed, and often therapeutic abortions were decided based on the whims of the doctors (almost always all white men) on these panels. Regardless of the path a woman chose, the first step was to learn whether or not she was actually pregnant because that gave her the critical information she needed to determine the course of her life. This $5 pregnancy test provided that.

Los Angeles was a developing city in the 1930s. Wide expanses were still farmland or open fields dotted with bungalow dwellings as streets were slowly being carved out. The more urbanized corners of the city housed squat office buildings lined along straight streets with the occasional tower punctuating the horizon. Figueroa Street, the site of one of the first clinics to commercially offer the pregnancy test, was in the heart of downtown Los Angeles. Already a car city in the 1930s, Figueroa Street was built to accommodate vehicles and was one of the more bustling streets in the new city. Doctor's offices and pharmacies were commonly housed in commercial buildings that helped create the discrete, anonymous environment promised by the ads in the *LA Times*. A gynecological clinic in the 1930s might have consisted of a few rooms: the doctor's office that housed a wide desk for consultations; an exam room with a folding bed and cabinets for tools; a waiting room for patients. And if the pregnancy test was offered on site with the promise of quick results, then a lab might also have been tucked out of sight to conceal the goriness of the pregnancy test.

The Toad Test

It would take the discovery of an aquatic South African toad's reproductive life, the *Xenopus laevis*, to put an end to the bloodshed behind every pregnancy test. In 1934, two South African scientists, Hillel Shapiro and Harry Zwarenstein, began experimenting with the clawed South African toad, a readily available and already-popular animal for scientific experiments. Their critical realization was that the Xenopus toad, as she's commonly known, only ovulates in the presence of a male toad. (Other frogs and toads ovulate spontaneously.) If you isolate female toads from male toads—even for months or years on end—they won't release their eggs, which are quite large and hard to miss. However, it was also discovered that if you inject the Xenopus with a pregnant woman's urine, the hCG in her urine would cause the eggs to drop. As long as the amount of urine injected into toads was small—and only a little bit of hCG seemed to trigger ovulation—the toads suffered no ill effect and could be repeatedly used for pregnancy tests. The Xenopus pregnancy test, as it came to be called, became a popular method for pregnancy testing for the next thirty years.

In 1938, Edward R. Elkan, a physician and researcher, published an article in a British medical journal celebrating the Xenopus pregnancy test, and it provides an intimate lens into the experience not only for the lab technician who performed the test but for the woman who took it. If a woman stopped by a clinic to receive instructions to prepare for the pregnancy test, here is what she might have been told:

1. Limit fluid intake on the day before collecting your urine.

2. Avoid taking all drugs for several days before the collection.

3. Collect approximately 6 ounces of morning urine in a clean but not necessarily sterile bottle.

4. Avoid drinking Vichy water or tea before producing urine.[8]

5. Bring bottle to clinic as soon as possible after collection.

Not following these instructions might produce invalid results. Results can be known in as little as five hours or as long as twelve hours.[9]

Elkan's observation that not an insignificant number of women drank tea or water to try to increase their urine output suggests that the women taking these tests felt at least a bit anxious about the process. And perhaps that's to be expected: in an era where propriety and discretion were highly valued, being asked to collect a very specific amount of an intimate bodily fluid that's normally quickly discarded and then to transport that bodily fluid in public might have been an uncomfortable if not embarrassing experience for many women. For them to still go through with the test, to share their urine, meant that they really must have wanted to know whether they were pregnant.

Once the urine arrived at the clinic, it was placed in cold storage until it was injected into the toad. Then, if the toad dropped at least five of its little half-black, half-white, round and gelatinous eggs, much like caviar in texture, the pregnancy test was considered positive. If after twelve hours, no eggs or only one or two eggs were dropped then the test was considered negative. The black-and-white mottled toads lived in large aquariums, and were isolated in their own jars each time a test was taken. Although they were allowed to rest between tests, they could be used repeatedly with seemingly no harm. In the US, the Xenopus test proved so successful that if a woman had a pregnancy test between 1944 and the mid-1960s, there's a good chance a toad—and then later other species of frogs—was involved. In California, an industry emerged for pregnancy testing with toads, and new businesses like the California Xenopus Laevis Exchange on Ventura Boulevard in Studio City opened, which was perhaps not coincidentally located conveniently close to Hollywood and its movie studios:

a legal pregnancy test could be followed by an illegal abortion.[10]

The adoption of the Xenopus test in the US did have some setbacks, especially during World War II when collecting toads from South Africa proved difficult.[11] Furthermore, the test wasn't foolproof and false negatives were more common than with the Friedman test. Still, when two American scientists introduced the Xenopus test in 1942 at the American Medical Association Conference, the media attention was overwhelmingly positive.[12] Newspapers proclaimed that a "perfect pregnancy test" had been found.[13] In 1947, some doctors realized that injecting several species of male toads and frogs with a pregnant woman's urine caused them to ejaculate. A number of different amphibian species were used for these procedures, from the South American male toad, the *Bufo marinus* (now known as the *Rhinella marina*), to the North American male frog, *Rana pipiens*.[14] Even though these American animals were easier to obtain than the *Xenopus*, identifying the sperm in their urine required a microscope. More problematically, sometimes the frogs and toads ejaculated for no reason at all, especially during their breeding months.[15] While toads and frogs allowed doctors to confirm the presence of hCG in a woman's urine without slaughtering an animal, it was still an imperfect and messy system. There was clearly a demand for a reliable pregnancy test, but the methods to detect hCG needed to be improved.

What exactly is hCG, this magical hormone that appears in the bodily fluids of pregnant women? The study of hormones, endocrinology, is relatively new. The study of hormones related to pregnancy, reproductive endocrinology, is even newer. The word "hormone" itself wasn't coined until the early twentieth century by Ernest Starling from the Greek word "ormao," which means to excite or stir up. Hormones do precisely that: they cause systems in the body to move into action; they create change. In pregnancy, hCG is produced by the placenta, and it's critical to stimulating the body to create another hormone, progesterone, without which a pregnancy cannot be maintained. The discovery that hCG was unique to pregnancy and could be found in urine is what initially led to a reliable laboratory pregnancy test; the developing fields of immunology and endocrinology that were experimenting with the various uses of antibodies, including hCG antibodies, are what finally resulted in a test that didn't rely on killing animals or keeping them alive in aquariums.

Hemagglutination Inhibition

In 1960, Leif Wide and Carl Gemzell, two Swedish doctors, announced their hemagglutination inhibition test. The word "hemagglutinate" describes the binding of red blood cells, and this test diagnosed pregnancy by looking for whether blood cells were binding or inhibited from binding based on the presence of hCG in a woman's urine. (As I'll explain later, pregnancy was indicated when the cells were inhibited from binding.) When their experiments for diagnosing pregnancy were successful, Wide and Gemzell immediately knew the test would garner consumer interest. In fact, the article they published in 1960, "An Immunological Pregnancy Test," ended with the note that Organon, the company that employed Meg Crane seven years later, would be developing a laboratory pregnancy test based on their discovery.[16]

Sure enough, within a few short years after 1960, if a woman received a pregnancy test, it was increasingly likely that she was given the hemagglutination inhibition test, first marketed by Organon as Prognosticon and processed in their labs. Unlike today's pregnancy tests that give a clear yes or no answer, or even unlike the rabbit or toad test which similarly gave fairly direct results, the hemagglutination inhibition test was read by looking for clumping cells after a woman's urine was combined with a specially prepared serum made of dried sheep blood coated in hCG antibodies and rabbit hCG antibodies made in labs. If enough clumping was seen, the woman was likely pregnant, and the positive result would show up like a reddish circle. Sometimes, however, false positives or false negatives arose if the test was administered improperly or if it was administered at the wrong time of a woman's cycle. The hormones women produce during menopause could also interfere with the results. Women with irregular cycles or women who couldn't remember the date of their last period could possibly get an incorrect result if the test was administered during another time in their cycle. Still, this technology made laboratory pregnancy testing significantly less expensive because it eliminated the need for animal-based pregnancy tests and therefore could be far more routine.

By the mid-1960s, confirming pregnancy using this laboratory pregnancy test, and eventually other tests based on this science, became a common practice when a woman went to see her doctor after a missed period. The procedure was even simple enough that it would eventually be packaged for home use, and it would form the basis of all home pregnancy tests for two decades. Even when the first American home pregnancy test, e.p.t., was released in 1978, seventeen years after Wide and Gemzell's essay was published, it still used this same rather clunky technology. It would take a number of innovations and discoveries to change that. Judith Vaitukaitis, a young National Institutes of Health (NIH) scientist, led the way in one avenue by improving the test's ability to identify and measure hCG.

Judith Vaitukaitis and beta-hCG

When Judith Vaitukaitis entered the field of reproductive endocrinology in the 1960s, very little was understood about how hormones worked and their exact role in reproduction or cancers of the reproductive system. It was known, however, that there are only a few circumstances under which a non-pregnant body will produce hCG, all of them signaling something is wrong: reproductive cancers. Vaitukaitis's goal was to find better ways to measure the production of hCG in a woman's body as an indicator of early cancer. She didn't intend to lead the way for an improved home pregnancy test, but that's exactly what happened.

In 1950, when Vaitukaitis was ten years old, the US saw a steep decline in the number of women who entered medical school. In fact, there were fewer women in medical school in 1950 than there were in 1900. When Vaitukaitis completed her medical degree in 1966, women comprised less than nine percent of doctors, and it was even more unusual that she chose to go into research rather than a practice. But Vaitukaitis's career in science and medicine was going to be anything but usual. She entered Tufts University in 1958, the year the university steeply increased its tuition, thus limiting the number of students from lower socio-economic backgrounds. At the same time, Tufts had a vibrant history of co-education, and it started admitting women in the late nineteenth century—well before many of its peer institutions. Vaitukaitis chose to major in the hard sciences—chemistry and biology—which meant that in many of her classes she was the only white woman in a room full of mostly white men. Later, at Boston University's medical school, in a class of 70 students, she was one of five women. At every stage of her career from then on this would almost always be the case. But Vaitukaitis wasn't bothered. When a fellow medical student told her that if it wasn't for her, he'd be at the top of the class, she responded, "Tough! Why don't you work harder?" Working hard was something Vaitukaitis did well.

As she told Sarah Leavitt, a historian and curator for the NIH, who interviewed her in 2003 for an interactive website about the pregnancy test's history, "it was a man's world. But I was so used to it."[17]

By the time Vaitukaitis graduated from medical school in 1970 she knew she wanted to pursue a career in research, but then, as now, positions were competitive and they were especially competitive for women. A mentor suggested she pursue reproductive endocrinology because, as a new field, there might be fewer people competing. At the same time, there might be more to lose because the future of the field was still unclear. Vaitukaitis followed this suggestion and found that endocrinology appealed to her sensibility: hormones were something that could be objectively measured, and increasingly, scientists were discovering better tools to measure them. She took the chance to be part of this work and accepted a postdoctoral position at the NIH in Washington, DC that was supposed to last for at most six months. She stayed for five and a half years.

The hours in the lab were long. She would work from 6 a.m. until 11 p.m. She even came in on weekend afternoons after playing golf, one of her only hobbies. Because funding for such a new field was tight, she often had no lab technicians to assist her and did all the technical and detail-oriented work herself. But the work was exciting. Later she would call it the "most fun time of my life" and add that if she had been independently wealthy she "would have done it for nothing." Almost immediately she started working on an answer to what on the surface seems like a relatively simple question: How could she find a way to better measure hCG? The hormone hCG, remember, is produced by the placenta in pregnancy, and more rarely, it's produced by some cancers of the reproductive system. A treatment had been found for choriocarcinoma, a cancer that can be sometimes found in the uterus, ovaries, or testes. And yet in order to treat this cancer, doctors needed a noninvasive method to first confirm it. When Vaitukaitis began her research the main tests used were what scientists call bioassays—tests that depend on live animals. And it was the same test used to confirm pregnancy: the Xenopus frog. Vaitukaitis wanted a better test, one that could identify the presence of hCG without the use of animals, which, besides being messy, were also far more inaccurate and expensive than using a radioimmunoassay, a tool that had been invented in the late 1950s to measure hormones like insulin more accurately and exactly. Radioimmunoassays use radioactive isotopes, usually iodine, to measure the level of a hormone in the patient's blood (or urine). However, endocrinologists before Vaitukaitis struggled to successfully create a radioimmunoassay for measuring hCG.

Vaitukaitis had a plan. But first, she needed lots of urine, and ideally some would have significant levels of hCG in it. Fortunately for Vaitukaitis she stumbled upon the perfect group, a group so perfect they would lead her to the results she needed: infertile women who were coming to the NIH to seek an experimental treatment that would help them get pregnant. The experimental treatment overlapped with

Vaitukaitis's work because it was discovered that ovulation could be triggered in some women if they were injected with a combination of hCG and other reproductive hormones (much like how hCG triggered the ovaries in mice, rabbits, and toads). However, Vaitukaitis also worried that in the process of treatment these women were receiving too much hCG, which could overstimulate their ovaries, and she wanted to find a way to detect this before their first missed period.

Two years later, in 1972, Vaitukaitis found it. The now classic essay she published has a mouthful of a name that's nevertheless quite descriptive: "A radioimmunoassay which specifically measures human chorionic gonadotropin in the presence of human luteinizing hormone."[18] Like almost all scientists, Vaitukaitis didn't work alone. Yet, as Glenn Braunstein and Griff Ross, her two co-authors, agreed, she would be the lead author for this article because it was her foundational work that led the way to the discovery. The eight-page essay with lots of charts and descriptions of different hormones and compounds describes the procedure Vaitukaitis used to isolate and measure hCG by combining it with different substances. Vaitukaitis's most critical contribution was her discovery that the beta-subunit of hCG—or beta-hCG—could be isolated and measured separately from the whole hCG molecule. The radioimmunoassay Vaitukaitis, Braunstein, and Ross created was both sensitive and accurate, and results could be reliably read more quickly than in the bioassays that relied on animals. At the time, Vaitukaitis didn't imagine her discovery would lead to a technology that could be used at home, but she was aware that it would improve on the methods used to test for pregnancy. Still, her work was not patented, and she never received a dime for her discoveries—beyond, of course, her salary for working at the NIH.

The title of Vaitukaitis's groundbreaking essay points to what was most exciting about her discovery for scientists, though it might sound hopelessly obscure to other readers: she discovered a way to measure hCG in the presence of human luteinizing hormone. This other hormone, which is critical for reproduction as well, is often shortened to LH, and unlike hCG, it's normally present in everyone, regardless of sex. In people with testes, it triggers the production of testosterone, and in people with ovaries it triggers ovulation. In fact, ovulation tests, which were modeled after the pregnancy test years after its development, work by detecting rising levels of LH in urine. LH and hCG are also molecularly very similar, and the biggest roadblock to developing a radioimmunoassay for pregnancy testing was finding a way to distinguish between LH and hCG in urine or blood.[19] Isolating beta-hCG from hCG, which consists of two compounds now labeled the alpha and beta subunits, was key, because the beta-subunit is molecularly distinct from LH while the alpha-subunit is nearly identical. Finding a way to measure beta-hCG in isolation eventually led to the more accurate home tests developed in the 1980s, which replaced the earlier, more prone-to-error tests that were never as popular.

Today, home pregnancy tests can detect pregnancy up to six days before a missed period. In part, Vaitukaitis's discovery led to this breakthrough. While it would take several other technological innovations to make the home pregnancy test more user friendly, Vaitukaitis brought the home pregnancy test one step closer to the object we know today. As a *New York Times* article published in December 1973 (the same year *Roe v. Wade* legalized abortion) recognized, a pregnancy test that allowed women to detect their pregnancies even before a missed period could make abortion more accessible.[20] Although home pregnancy tests like e.p.t. didn't begin using this technology until the mid-1980s, once they did, the home pregnancy test was transformed into an object that gave women results with an immediacy and accuracy never accessible to them before. From the moment a period was missed, women could determine whether they were pregnant. And the chance of error was minuscule because now the home pregnancy test could detect even tiny amounts of hCG imperceptible to the earlier versions of the test. This kind of direct knowledge, well before any symptom of early pregnancy might appear, was almost magical.

Still, a lot had to happen before the pregnancy test transformed how we learn about pregnancy, and the process was not always linear. The laboratory pregnancy tests advertised in various Los Angeles newspapers, for example, petered out by the late 1930s, around the same time California began cracking down on the illegal abortion industry. An occasional post in the classified section could still be found in the early 1940s, advertising both pregnancy and Wasserman tests, which was a popular test for syphilis. By the 1950s they were gone. However, with the invention of the laboratory test that didn't require an animal, the pregnancy test became more commonly used by doctors, and this meant that in the 1960s and 70s women started expecting that their pregnancies could be confirmed—but only under the supervision of their doctor and more often than not, only if they were married. In the United States, it would take several more decades before women would be given access to this knowledge without the mediating gaze of a doctor or medical practitioner.

The early history of the pregnancy test we use today had multiple false starts, and there were various tests along that way that were briefly lauded as revolutionary, only to later reveal that they in fact rarely gave accurate results. After all, since a pregnancy test usually only has two answers—positive or negative—it will be correct some of the time by chance. Yet, if we find the twentieth-century pregnancy test mired with false prophecy, the tests that came before sound like inventions born of fairy tales.

3 URINE AND BLOOD

When Selmar Aschheim and Bernhard Zondek invented the first accurate pregnancy test in 1927, they drew on a long history of using urine to test for pregnancy. Why did people look at urine for signs of pregnancy? For one, medicine has a long tradition of using urine as a diagnostic tool to assess the health and wellbeing of people and animals. During the Middle Ages in Europe, urine became doctors' primary method for examining the overall health of their patients. A special tool, the matula, a clear bulbous glass, became as synonymous with medicine in the Middle Ages as the stethoscope is today. In these glasses, urine was examined for its color, consistency, odor, and content, and depending on these factors, doctors gave a diagnosis of the patient's humors, which were said to determine the state of a patient's health.[1] Pregnancy was just one of many conditions that supposedly could be diagnosed through a close inspection of urine, and thus these doctors were aptly named "piss prophets" for their foretelling.

Using urine for diagnostic purposes has an even longer tradition, however. Medical practitioners in ancient Greece,

Rome, and Egypt believed that urine was produced by the liver and then excreted by the kidneys and bladder, and they relied on it to diagnose health issues. Urine was seen to regularly breach the boundaries of the human body, from inside to out, and therefore, could serve as a lens to understand what was happening in places the human eye couldn't see. Doctors in the Western world continued to rely on urine to assess a patient's health well into the eighteenth century. Pregnancy, like many other conditions that are difficult to diagnose in early stages, was considered as one among those that could be revealed by an analysis of urine.

The earliest evidence of urinary pregnancy tests are documented on an Egyptian papyrus from 1350 BC, which is now called the "Berlin Medical Papyrus," held by the Egyptian Museum of Berlin. The test involved filling two bags, one with barley seeds and the other with wheat. The woman was to urinate daily on each of these bags. If the seeds in the barley bag sprouted, it meant she was pregnant with a male child, and if the wheat seeds sprouted, it meant a female child. If neither sprouted, then she was not pregnant at all.[2] A similar test to determine fertility was described in a medieval Arabic text from the tenth century by Aly Abul Abbas el Magousy. In this version of the test, both a childless man and woman urinated on seven bags each of barley, wheat, and beans. If one of the bags sprouted after seven days, it meant that the person who urinated on the bag was not the cause of the couple's infertility.

While these pregnancy and fertility tests may seem implausible to a contemporary reader, in 1963 researchers took them seriously enough to test the science. Three Egyptian doctors and researchers co-authored a study duplicating the Egyptian pregnancy test methods. To their surprise, they discovered that a pregnant woman's urine could encourage the germination of both barley and wheat. In contrast, the seeds watered with urine from a woman who wasn't pregnant did not sprout at all. Still, they cautioned that in some cases, seeds watered with a pregnant woman's urine did not sprout, and so this method for pregnancy testing could not be considered determinative. They found no correlation between the sex of the fetus and whether barley or wheat sprouted. As they concluded, "when growth occurs, the urine is presumably that of a pregnant woman, but the reverse is not necessarily true."[3]

In the centuries that followed, there were other tests that used urine to check for pregnancy. Albertus Magnus, a German Catholic Dominican Friar, who was born around 1200 and dabbled in medicine as well as philosophy, believed that milk poured into a glass of a pregnant woman's urine would float. In the early sixteenth century, Jacob Rueff, a Zurich-born physician who published the well-regarded text *The Expert Midwife*, believed that one method for diagnosing pregnancy was to place an iron needle in a cup of urine overnight. If by morning the needle was covered in black spots, it meant the woman was pregnant. In the seventeenth century, Cornelius Solingen, a Dutch physician, advised women to mix their urine with wine, and if the mixture "becomes turbid as though beans had stewed in it, the woman is pregnant."[4] Experiments using urine to determine pregnancy continued into the early twentieth century. In 1933, it was believed that female Japanese Bitterling fish injected with a pregnant woman's urine released eggs. A big problem with this test was that these fish were hard to handle and prone to biting.

One of the most historically significant urine-based pregnancy tests came from the work of Regina Kapeller-Adler, a Jewish-Austrian biochemist who worked at the University of Vienna until 1938, when she was forced to flee to Scotland after the Nazi occupation of Austria expelled all Jewish scientists from their academic posts. Kapeller-Adler came from an observant Jewish home, and she was unusual among women of her time for pursuing a doctorate in science and continuing her research after she married and had a child. As a Jewish woman in Vienna in the 1930s, however, it had been almost impossible for her to find work, and so she agreed to take an unpaid laboratory position at the university so she could pursue her research. In 1934, to much acclaim, the Viennese press announced that Kapeller-Adler had found a new test for pregnancy. She believed that in early pregnancy women secreted more histidine, an amino acid found in various foods, in their urine, and so she developed a chemical test that was able to identify histidine in urine. Her hope was that this discovery could then be translated into a routine pregnancy test that didn't rely on a live animal.[5] While a histidine pregnancy test ultimately never came to fruition, in 1939, the science was promising enough that Kapeller-Adler was offered a research position at the University of Edinburgh, and this allowed her, her husband, and her four-year-old daughter to escape Nazi persecution. She continued a productive research career in biochemistry as she worked on the possibility of a chemically based pregnancy test at a time when other researchers and doctors relied on live animals.

Nineteenth-Century Signs

By the nineteenth century, most Western doctors had stopped using urine to diagnose pregnancy. As Ann Oakley, a historian of women's reproductive medicine, documents, in 1834 the physician James Blundell wryly noted that, "The most certain mode of knowing whether a woman be in a state of gestation or not is by waiting till the term of nine months is complete."[6] Despite this doctor's seeming reluctance to diagnose pregnancy before the birth of the baby, other Victorian doctors occasionally agreed to physically examine their patients to determine pregnancy. Since touching female patients, even on their abdomen, was considered improper, women's noses, eyes, and mouths were sometimes examined for what were considered telltale signs of pregnancy. Occasionally, Oakley explains, upper-class Victorian women were given a physical evaluation, including a vaginal examination, but in these cases, they were first sedated with opiates because it was considered too embarrassing for both the woman and doctor to do this examination with the woman conscious.[7]

In the US, the well-regarded physician Charles Meigs, who authored an authoritative gynecological textbook in 1856, acknowledged the difficulty of diagnosing pregnancy. He recommended either using a long stethoscope or the bare ear to listen for the fetus's heartbeat, but he cautioned that it is usually hard to hear anything definitive before the fourth month of pregnancy. He also described a way of touching a woman's womb through her vaginal walls to see if it is enlarged but discouraged most doctors from using this method because it required a woman to undress from her waist down. By the late nineteenth century, more gynecologists were willing to internally examine a woman to determine pregnancy, and a number of "signs," all named after the male doctors who first described them, were coined. There was "Hegar's Sign" that required a doctor to insert two fingers into a woman's vagina and place his hand on her abdomen to palpate the uterus to feel whether it had softened in such a way to indicate pregnancy. This softening supposedly could be felt between the fourth and twelfth weeks of pregnancy. "Chadwick's Sign" looked for a change in color to the cervix, vagina, and labia, indicative of pregnancy. "Goodell's Sign" described the softening of the cervix, which often happens by the sixth week of pregnancy, and is still noted by obstetricians in prenatal exams. Still, because all these tests were considered to be invasive and intimate, it was rare for physicians to employ them unless medically necessary. As the historian Lara Freidenfelds notes, even by the mid-twentieth century, most pregnancy guides told women to wait until they missed two periods before suspecting pregnancy. At this point, women would be between two and three months pregnant and begin experiencing other common signs of early pregnancy like nausea, frequent urination, and darkening of the nipples.[8]

The Era of Invasive Pregnancy Tests

Through the early twentieth century, pregnancy diagnosis continued to be considered as either something only a woman could ascertain herself or something done with the help of the rarely done physical examination by a doctor. Yet, in just a few short decades, with the invention of the A-Z laboratory pregnancy test in 1927, scientists, doctors, and businesspeople recognized that a robust market for a reliable pregnancy test (or a somewhat reliable pregnancy test) existed, and there was no shortage of new inventions to test for pregnancy. Some of these methods had questionable science behind them, and others might have some scientific basis but disregarded the harm women might experience as a result. For example, in 1941 the *Los Angeles Times* enthusiastically reported on a new pregnancy test that injected colostrum into a woman's forearm to test for pregnancy. Colostrum is the thin, yellowish liquid women produce by late pregnancy and shortly after childbirth to feed newborns. In this version of the pregnancy test, colostrum was collected from women who were twenty-eight weeks pregnant and injected into the arms of women who suspected they might be pregnant. None of the articles describing this procedure noted the potential danger of injecting a foreign bodily fluid into a woman's arm. This test, which came to be called the "Q-test," was read by looking for a reddish welt, much like a mosquito bite, to appear on a woman's arm in response. If a welt appeared within thirty-minutes and grew in size over the next few hours, a woman was considered not pregnant. If no welt appeared, or if only a small welt appeared that hadn't grown, the woman was diagnosed as pregnant. News reports of this test described it as helpful in rural areas where access to pregnancy tests using live animals was not readily available.[9]

The doctors who devised the Q-test claimed that it was based on an allergic reaction that was absent in pregnant women because their bodies didn't react to colostrum as a foreign substance. Before trying colostrum, these same doctors had injected various other substances into women's arms, including breast milk, cow milk, and placental tissue in hopes of discovering a substance that could be used as a pregnancy test. None of these worked, until, according to their trials, they found injected colostrum to correctly diagnose pregnancy in 98 percent of cases and to correctly diagnose non-pregnancy in 96 percent of cases. (Later clinical studies would disprove these results and show a much higher rate of false positives and false negatives.) Still, there are many unanswered questions about the use of colostrum as a pregnancy test. The two doctors who devised this test specified that the colostrum could only be collected from women who were pregnant for the first time.[10] Colostrum collected from women in their second or third pregnancies supposedly did not give as accurate results. Yet their article, published in 1941, says nothing about the women who had colostrum extracted from their breasts at twenty-eight weeks of pregnancy, which surely would have been an unpleasant and unusual procedure. Were these women told why their colostrum was collected? Were they compensated? Did they have the opportunity to consent? The study is silent on these questions. The Q-test would continue to circulate as a pregnancy test into the 1950s, and advertisements for it can be found in various newspapers until it eventually petered out. Perhaps it was found to be unreliable; perhaps women started objecting to having their colostrum extracted; or perhaps women didn't like having another woman's bodily fluid inserted into their arm, no matter how small the amount.[11]

Or, perhaps the Q-test was just replaced with another invasive pregnancy test that saw its popularity rise in the late 1950s: the hormonal pregnancy test. Starting in 1949, doctors began experimenting with injecting various hormones and even chemical compounds into women's bloodstream to test for pregnancy. The earliest tests used estrone, a form of estrogen now linked to cancers. Women were given three injections of estrone in a doctor's office over a period of five days. If a woman wasn't pregnant, she would begin menstruating within twenty-four hours. If she was pregnant, then she wouldn't bleed. The test was lauded as a way to diagnose pregnancy without the use of a lab and live animals.[12]

Doctors continued to experiment with other injected substances that might test for pregnancy. In 1952, the chemical compound stigmonene bromide was used in a similar way.[13] Women received several shots of this chemical, which was later used in cleaning products, and if within days they started bleeding they were diagnosed as not pregnant. Over the next few years, doctors experimented with various hormonal injections, combining different forms of estrogen and progesterone and advertising these procedures, both as a way to test for pregnancy and to cure amenorrhea, a condition that describes women who have stopped menstruating for reasons other than pregnancy or menopause. There's a long history of women taking various herbs to bring on their bleeding, whether because their amenorrhea was caused by a medical condition or because they wanted to end an early pregnancy. The line between menstruation that has stopped because of pregnancy and menstruation that stopped for other physiological reasons can be blurry, and it was especially so before the mid-nineteenth century. Following this history then, it's not surprising to learn that soon the injectable pregnancy tests morphed into hormonal tablets prescribed by doctors when women's menstruation had ceased for inexplicable reasons.

In the US, these hormonal tablets were sold under different brand names, but the two most popular were Pro-Duosterone and Gestest. Both were made up of progesterone and estrogen, the same hormones that were being used to create birth control pills in this era as well. Pro-Duosterone was the first hormonal tablet test introduced to Americans in 1958 and consisted of small, pink tablets that were advertised as less expensive and more accurate than the rabbit, frog, and mouse tests that were more readily available. Women were instructed to take four of these pink pills, no bigger than aspirin, per day for three days, one at each meal and one at bedtime. If after the third day, they started bleeding it meant they were not pregnant. However, if a week had passed with no bleeding, it meant a pregnancy diagnosis.[14] Gestest was released just a few short years after Pro-Duosterone, and its main advantage was that women only had to take two tablets each day for two days, thus reducing the number of pills and time needed to administer the test.

Since neither of these tests were available over the counter, women had to ask their doctor for a prescription. Doctors were instructed to closely monitor patients for their reactions to the hormones and early medical articles from the 1960s praised the tablets for causing few side effects in women. (Given that the pills contained forms of estrogen and progesterone in large doses, similar to the morning-after-pill and early versions of the birth control pill, which are known to cause various side effects, including nausea, vomiting, and anxiety, it's hard to believe that there were no side effects. It's much easier to believe that the researchers studying women in these trials discounted these side effects as trivial.) Announcing Gestest's introduction to the market, one Alabama newspaper unabashedly titled a 1961 widely syndicated article about the pills, "Woman is Her Own Guinea Pig in More Accurate Pregnancy Test" and reassured women that the pills "play a dual role": if a woman is pregnant, then the progesterone protects the pregnancy, and if she's not, then the pills encourage menstruation to begin "just as Nature planned it."[15]

These hormonal pregnancy tests were increasingly popular in the 1960s, first as alternatives to the animal tests, which were expensive and ethically questionable, and then to the hemagglutination inhibition tests—the first laboratory tests that didn't require an animal—because they could be done at home, even if they required a doctor's prescription. One article quotes a doctor who estimated that between 5,000 and 7,500 women in New York State took hormonal pregnancy tests each year.[16] However, two controversies eventually led to the pill being pulled off the market. Almost from the moment the pills were introduced, women began telling each other that these pills were more than just a pregnancy test and that they could induce miscarriage. And while the pills' manufacturers insisted this wasn't true, rumors persisted that would eventually be partly vindicated by studies in the 1970s.[17] After all, the morning-after pill, another hormonal pill meant to prevent early pregnancy, contains a similar mix of hormones. Even more controversially, by 1972 some studies indicated various disabilities in babies whose mothers took these pills.[18] While these studies continue to be controversial to this day, at that point in time enough controversy had followed the hormonal pregnancy test for the FDA to pull its approval in 1975.[19] Intentionally or not, the elimination of this popular pregnancy test created an opening for Warner-Lambert to gain approval for its first home pregnancy test for the American market in 1976.

The desire to know whether you're pregnant is strong, strong enough that you might be willing to ingest or inject substances to get answers. Many doctors didn't hesitate asking women to subject their bodies to invasive tests or take large doses of hormones. The medical establishment had its own interests in diagnosing early pregnancy. The earlier a woman was diagnosed as pregnant, the earlier she would seek medical attention, which didn't always lead to better outcomes for women in this era.

4 THE STICK

The stick-shaped home pregnancy test is so commonly used today that anyone reading this book can likely conjure up an image of this object sold in your corner drugstore. It's become commonplace, and, for many people, something to throw away once it's served its purpose. Even as it might be one of the most emotionally laden objects in our lives, it's one that in the twenty-first-century US we've come to take for granted. Yet, the science it took to develop this object is so complex and took many years of advances in biotechnology. When I began this research, I had no idea that I would soon need crash courses in immunology, endocrinology, biochemistry, and even paper manufacturing. And although histories of the pregnancy test sometimes credit this or that person for its invention, in truth, not one person can claim full responsibility because so many different fields of knowledge went into its making. It's an impressive piece of technology, especially for an object that can now be bought for just a couple of dollars.

Two of the most important turning points marking the sexual revolution in the 1960s and 1970s, which transformed

American women's sex lives by making sex without the fear of pregnancy or children possible, are the birth control pill, which came on the American market in 1960, and legal abortion through *Roe v. Wade* in 1973. One could argue that the wide-scale introduction of the home pregnancy test in 1978 was equally as important because it gave women control over their reproductive choices without the eyes of a judgmental and patronizing doctor. So why has the invention of the home pregnancy test been mostly left out of these histories? Why has the pregnancy test not been given credit for transforming women's sex lives and giving them control in ways never available before?

When e.p.t. released the first home pregnancy test on the American market in 1978, the company latched onto changing sexual mores to promote its product. Its first ad called the test "a little revolution," staking the company's claim in what, by 1978, was clearly a dramatic shift in what was sexually possible for women. Yet, American women were not convinced at first. The reception for the first home pregnancy tests was lukewarm, and there wasn't really a revolution at all because the vast majority of women ignored the new home tests. When I started writing this book I was swayed by e.p.t.'s argument that they had a part in a small revolution for women's sex lives. After all, as I discuss in the previous three chapters, the home pregnancy test gave women direct access to knowledge that had for decades been mediated through a paternalistic medical culture. In this chapter, however, I want to complicate that narrative.[1]

Why were American women slow to adopt the home pregnancy test? It's hard to untangle all the reasons because there were several potential factors. For one, despite a robustly positive advertising campaign by e.p.t. and the home pregnancy tests that followed (Answer, Daisy 2, and others), some laboratories began their own advertising campaigns in the same women's magazines suggesting that the home pregnancy test was unreliable. Wampole Laboratories, for example, which processed thousands of pregnancy tests every year for doctors' offices, took out full-page ads proclaiming that women "should leave pregnancy testing in the hands of professionals." These ads argued that laboratory-based pregnancy tests were more accurate and could be done earlier after a missed period. Perhaps to avoid appearing sexist, their ad featured a woman technician in a white coat handling the laboratory pregnancy test.

Even though the introduction of the home pregnancy test in the US was a long-awaited development, the fact that it had been available in Canada and Europe for almost eight years already meant there was little fanfare when brought to American pharmacies. The glossy women's magazines didn't feature any major articles about this new product and what it might mean for women's reproductive lives. A few advice columnists responded tepidly to questions about the reliability of the new home pregnancy test, always advising women to visit their doctors because a negative test might not be accurate and a positive test required medical advice about next steps. Though the women's magazine *Redbook* published a short announcement about the home pregnancy test's availability in drugstores as early as January 1978, it was not given much prominence or discussed in depth. And medical journals from the time suggested that American doctors were skeptical about the home pregnancy test's reliability.[2]

Therefore, despite the extensive advertising campaigns in magazines, newspapers, and on TV by the manufacturers of the new home pregnancy test kits, women were receiving enough advice to dissuade them from purchasing tests, which were costly and still viewed as unreliable. It's quite likely many American women didn't see the home pregnancy test as worth the cost when they had become accustomed to obtaining pregnancy results from a doctor's office.

Not Accurate and Not Reliable

Was it true that the 1978 version of the home pregnancy test wasn't reliable? The answer is complicated. The first home pregnancy tests released on the American market used the same biotechnology as the kits sold in Canada in the early 1970s. Several were even modeled on Meg Crane's 1969 design. This test could only be used nine days after a missed period, and sometimes even that was too early. Most doctors advised not using the test until after two missed periods. The test also needed to be left for two hours in an absolutely still environment with no direct sunlight or the results could be invalidated. Importantly, it wasn't sensitive enough to detect the smaller amounts of hCG produced by an ectopic pregnancy, a point emphasized by some women's magazines to discourage women from using the home test. At the same time, the technology for detecting pregnancy earlier and more reliably in a lab had advanced since 1970, even though the home test hadn't. By early 1977, magazines and newspapers printed stories about the new radio-receptor pregnancy test available with a doctor's prescription and through labs.[3] *Good Housekeeping* told its readers that this test could be offered "while you wait," and that it was more sensitive and accurate than any test available before, including the ones soon to be sold over the counter in pharmacies. While the 1977 radio-receptor pregnancy test differed from the test Judith Vaitukaitis and her team at the National Institutes of Health developed, it similarly used radioactive elements to measure levels of hCG in a woman's urine. Given the special equipment and skills needed to work with radioactivity, there was no way this test was ever going to be used outside a lab.

Glenn Braunstein, who co-authored papers with Vaitukaitis, explained to me over the phone that three advancements were needed for the technology they invented to detect beta-hCG to be implemented in the home pregnancy test. It was only after these technologies were brought together that the home pregnancy test became as accurate and reliable as the test we know today. And it was this technology that ultimately allowed women to test for pregnancy as soon as they missed their period—if not before—in the now-familiar wand home pregnancy tests. None of these technologies were invented specifically for the pregnancy test, but like Braunstein's cancer research on hCG, they unintentionally transformed it.

First, let me take a step back to explain again, but this time in a bit more detail, the science behind the earliest laboratory pregnancy tests because it's critical to understanding how the newer generation of pregnancy tests differed. Every reliable laboratory pregnancy test ever invented is considered an immunological test because it relies on testing for hCG with the use of antibodies. The early versions of the test, including the home pregnancy test, extracted hCG antibodies with the help of rabbits. Because hCG is a foreign substance for rabbits (it comes from humans, after all), when they're injected with hCG, their bodies produce antibodies to it. Scientists extracted the rabbit's blood with the hCG antibodies, separated out the antibodies, dried them, and added small amounts to test tubes. Another packet of dried sheep blood cells coated with hCG (also extracted from human beings, of course) was supplied. When distilled water was added to the dried blood along with urine from a pregnant woman (which would have hCG in it), the antibodies would bond to the hCG present, and when the sheep blood cells were added they would have nothing to bond with and therefore a ring would appear at the bottom of the test tube indicating pregnancy. If there was no hCG present in a woman's urine, the sheep cells would react to the rabbit antibodies and there would be no ring. Even though these tests were meant to replace pregnancy tests that relied on animals—like the rabbit, mouse, frog, and toad tests—they still depended on animal testing to produce the antibodies and blood cells necessary for the chemical reaction that would indicate pregnancy.

The invention of monoclonal antibodies in 1975 changed that. Monoclonal antibodies are artificially created antibodies using cell cultures that don't rely on lab animals. (The cell cultures are made by cloning cells, hence the name.) They can be duplicated over and over again in labs and are therefore more reliable, specific, and consistent than the method of creating hCG antibodies using rabbits. Monoclonal antibodies also eliminated the need to keep a regular supply of rabbits to produce rabbit antibodies for the tests.

The second important invention for the modern home pregnancy test, according to Braunstein, was the enzyme-led immunoassay, or ELISA (pronounced "eliza") in 1971. An ELISA is simply an assay—or test—that uses enzymes to detect a reaction between an antigen (like hCG or a coronavirus) and an antibody. ELISAs would transform pregnancy diagnosis, and they would soon be used to diagnose everything from the flu to HIV. In early 2020, the first Covid-19 detection tests were all ELISAs (as are most of the home kits). It was in 1976, however, that an ELISA for detecting hCG was created. ELISAs weren't invented with the home pregnancy test in mind, but they were used as a replacement for the radioimmunoassay because its reliance on radioactive substances made it a hazard for routine testing. The enzyme in the ELISA replaced the radioactive iodine as a means of measuring hCG because it similarly responds to the chemical reaction between the hCG antibodies and the presence of the hormone. If hCG was present in a woman's urine, hCG would bind to the antibodies in the test and the enzyme in the ELISA reacted by turning blue. No hCG, no binding, no color change.

By the mid-1980s, it seemed like a new kind of home pregnancy test was introduced to the American market each year. There was the test where you mixed your urine with a solution of monoclonal antibodies in a cup, and if the liquid stayed red you weren't pregnant. If it became clear, then you were. By 1984, e.p.t. announced that they had a new, improved test: the dipstick test for pregnancy. In this test, women could pee in a cup, mix in an enzyme solution, and then dip a stick in. If the tip of the stick turned blue (or pink in another version) they were pregnant. No color change, and they were not.[4] Advance, another home pregnancy test brand, quickly came out with their own version of an ELISA pregnancy test. In their test, results could be known in as little as thirty minutes, which seemed extraordinary compared to the two-hour waits necessary for the earlier tests.

Before the introduction of ELISA pregnancy tests, the market for home pregnancy tests barely grew in the US. The heads of pharmaceutical companies marketing the first home pregnancy tests had hoped their new products would radically change pregnancy diagnosis to create a new profitable market; instead, very little changed. By 1985, an executive for Warner-Lambert, the maker of e.p.t., noted that home pregnancy tests were purchased by only ten percent of possible users. However, he predicted that due to the new ELISA version of e.p.t., the market would grow exponentially.[5] He was right, although even then—and for some years after—it was still dominated by white, well-educated, married women.

Self-Diagnosis

The limited consumer market for home pregnancy tests wasn't by chance. While advertisements for home pregnancy tests emphasized the test's reliability and accuracy, the women featured in their ads were overwhelmingly white and conspicuously married. The manufacturers of these tests had a clear customer in mind. The first commercials for the dipstick pregnancy test, which appeared in November 1987, showed a white couple prominently wearing wedding bands. Warner-Lambert, the test's manufacturer, said the wedding bands were intentional but no moral message was intended. Since seventy percent of their consumers were married women, they were advertising to the audience they thought would most likely purchase their test. They didn't address why married women bought their product more readily.

We can speculate: there was the cost, for one. In 1984, the average pregnancy test cost an average of $10 (equivalent to about $25 in 2021), which was not exactly affordable. A 1982 study comparing the instructions for home pregnancy tests also found that they were not always easy to read. Some of the most popular home pregnancy tests, including e.p.t and Predictor, required an eighth- or ninth-grade reading level. The authors of this study suggested that many of the words used in the instructions relied on unfamiliar technical terms and that clarity could be improved.[6] Another 1986 study out of Milwaukee, Wisconsin found that women with no high school education and who were under twenty-one years old had a much higher error rate when taking home pregnancy tests.[7]

Increasingly, women's health clinics were also offering pregnancy tests on a sliding scale and openly advertising these services. A 1981 article in *Seventeen*, the popular magazine for teenage girls, encouraged its readers to go to Planned Parenthood if they suspected pregnancy and reassured them that Planned Parenthood never turned someone away if they couldn't pay.[8] Then, in the late 1970s, in response to *Roe v. Wade*, many anti-abortion clinics opened and found that by advertising free pregnancy testing in local newspapers and magazines they could draw women into their clinics. They intentionally hoped to attract pregnant women who were considering an abortion with the lure of free tests. The ads, however, rarely gave away these intentions, and many women who found the cost of a home pregnancy test prohibitive were likely attracted to these services only to discover that with a free pregnancy test came a coercive, often pseudoscientific lecture about the harms of abortion.

While there were cost barriers and other difficulties to accessing the pregnancy test, in time, the pregnancy test would upend a culture where women relied on an understanding of their reproductive bodies to diagnose pregnancy. In the mid-1970s, the medical anthropologist Brigitte Jordan volunteered in a women's health clinic that valued self-diagnosis for pregnancy and working with women to understand their bodies. She wanted to see how many women accurately diagnosed themselves as pregnant using bodily changes like a missed period, tender or enlarged breasts, and nausea. While she only worked with thirty-three women, she found that all but one woman correctly diagnosed herself as pregnant (or not) without the help of a pregnancy test. And yet, when Jordan called thirty doctors' offices pretending to be a woman whose period was a week late and who wanted an abortion, she found that none of them would take her word for it. They all insisted that the first thing she would need is a laboratory pregnancy test. For a contemporary reader, this stipulation on the part of doctors might sound like common sense. Of course doctors would want to confirm a pregnancy before performing an abortion. However, for centuries before the invention of the laboratory pregnancy test, women's own diagnosis of their pregnancy had often sufficed to induce an abortion. Jordan's study pointed to a change in this culture.

Jordan conducted her study before the home pregnancy test was available in the US so it's impossible to say how the availability of self-testing might have impacted her study. Still, she noted that the laboratory pregnancy test had become the new ubiquitous standard, ushering in what she termed "the medical model of pregnancy diagnosis."[9] Women's own conviction about what was happening to their bodies could no longer be trusted. In many ways, the pregnancy test, and even the home pregnancy test, expedited this process. Now, from the first day after a missed period, a woman could take a test that made her an "obstetric subject," whether she wanted an abortion or intended to seek prenatal care.[10] The pregnancy test might have given women more information about their bodies than ever before, but it came at the cost of a consumerist model of medical knowledge: there is a price to pay for learning about the inner workings of your body.

Furthermore, a pregnancy test, even a home pregnancy test, could be used coercively. An article from the *Ladies' Home Journal* published in 1979 reports on Terry Moore, a young white woman in jail for fifteen years for stealing a motorcycle. After being sexually pursued by a prison guard for several years, she agreed to have sex with him, and shortly after, she realized she was pregnant. When Terry confided in a friend about her pregnancy, word soon spread, and prison officials asked her to take a pregnancy test. She refused because she was worried she would be forced to have an abortion once her pregnancy was confirmed. Only after she was promised that she would not be punished for having sex with a guard and that she wouldn't be forced to have an abortion did she agree to a test. Her body and her pregnancy would no longer be under her full control. While Terry was temporarily allowed to have custody of her daughter after her birth, it wasn't clear by the article's end whether she would be forced to give up her daughter for adoption while she served the rest of her sentence.[11] Regardless, once her pregnancy was confirmed by a test, her body was closely monitored by prison officials and guards, and her freedom of movement was even further curtailed. Even if she didn't name it as such, Terry recognized that once she took that pregnancy test she became an "obstetric subject."

Accurate and Reliable

Improvements in-home pregnancy testing continued. In 1987, Whitehall Laboratories, based in England, released Clearblue One Step, a home pregnancy test that would be a game changer. By January 1988, the test would be marketed as Clearblue Easy in the US, and it was the first home pregnancy test shaped like today's familiar wands. Initially, advertisers compared them to pens. Clearblue, as its British name suggests, only required one step: women were instructed to hold the tip of the wand in their urine stream, cap it, and then—most wondrous of all—the results could be read in only three minutes. At the time of Clearblue's release, most tests required at least five steps and a wait time of anywhere from fifteen to thirty minutes. Clearblue's early advertisements in the US emphasized this difference. Their first advertisement showed a woman trying to read multi-stepped, complicated instructions with a perplexed look on her face with a mess of test tubes, Q-tips, a timer, and what might even be a spilled cup of urine in front of her. Their next ad presented a chart comparing Clearblue to all the leading home pregnancy test brands. Clearblue had the fewest pieces (just one!), the shortest wait time, and only one step. Accuracy wasn't sacrificed for this ease, as the ad highlighted. Clearblue was also the first pregnancy test to use the now-familiar shorthand for reading pregnancy tests: a negative pregnancy test showed one blue line; a positive pregnancy showed two.

Clearblue would eventually come to dominate the home pregnancy test markets in both the US and Europe, and it was thanks to a third invention: a porous nitrocellulose membrane, which created a lateral flow assay. In other words, scientists had found a way to improve on ELISAs by engineering strips of cellulose that absorbed liquid at the tip and then caused the liquid to flow laterally—or up the strip. This describes the technology of the paper inside every home pregnancy test wand today. With this new technology, scientists could adhere beta-hCG antibodies and the enzymes needed to read the results to the cellulose paper. (The antibodies and enzymes are literally sandwiched inside the paper.) Then, when the paper absorbs the urine it travels toward the antibodies. If there is hCG in the urine, a reaction occurs that's read by the enzymes as a color change, which in most early pregnancy tests appears as a second line. No reaction, and all the test takers would see is a first line, which was put there as a control so users could know the test was working. This control line was a clever innovation because in earlier pregnancy test kits women had no way of knowing whether a negative result meant they weren't pregnant or whether it meant the test just hadn't worked because a step was done incorrectly. As one early article celebrating this new test was titled, "New pregnancy test cuts out the chemistry lesson." Women could now test for pregnancy without the need to mix hormones and enzymes into a cup of urine. Furthermore, because this home pregnancy test looked for beta-hCG, it could be done as early as the first day after a missed period.[12]

Within a few years, almost all the leading home pregnancy test brands followed Clearblue's example and released their own wand-version of the home pregnancy test. Some brands also intentionally decided to change their advertising campaigns—not without controversy—to reach untapped markets. As one marketing journal noted in 1990, manufacturers of home pregnancy tests had kept their advertising fairly staid in order to "avoid some of the more delicate issues inherent in their products." As a result, they focused on "mature, upscale women who want to be pregnant," which the article calls "the least risky consumers." However, Carter-Wallace, which manufactured the Answer home pregnancy test and had recently acquired the company that made First Response, decided it would start marketing to college students and not assume in advertisements that a positive test was always good news. Their new slogan to target this younger age group of mostly single women was, "Until you know, nothing else matters."[13]

In 1991, the popular TV show *Murphy Brown* shocked audiences when Murphy, a single, successful, white newscaster, learns she's pregnant using, of course, a home pregnancy test. While some people credit the show with popularizing the home pregnancy test and showcasing its accuracy—Murphy takes multiple home tests hoping they might be wrong, but they all show the same result: positive— the show also demonstrated how the home pregnancy test might not be the most private way to discover a pregnancy. At the drugstore, she runs into her boss who notices her cart filled with home pregnancy tests. (She had decided to take more than a dozen to confirm her initial positive test.) Her boss panics because he doesn't see how an unmarried, pregnant news anchor could keep her job without public condemnation. Vice President Dan Quayle would later infamously criticize the fictional Murphy for "eroding family values" because she had premarital sex, and then chose to raise a child out of wedlock.[14] Murphy also openly considered an abortion on the show, much to some viewers' dismay. Regardless of whether *Murphy Brown* contributed to the popularization of the home pregnancy test or whether the show was a barometer of its increasing popularity, by the early 1990s, the market exploded. Between 1992 and 2004, the home pregnancy test market went from selling 750 million dollars of tests to 2.8 billion dollars.[15] Today in the US alone, it's estimated that 20 million women use a home pregnancy test each year.[16] As a result, most doctors now assume women will find out about their pregnancies using a test at home.

What changed? For one, while the name brands sold in stores are still relatively expensive, women can now buy generic brands in local drugstores or online for as little as just a couple of dollars. The advertising campaigns also shifted: pharmaceutical companies began advertising the test to a wider audience, including younger single women and women of color. And in the twenty-first century, as the next section of this book will explore, the home pregnancy test became the standard way to diagnose pregnancy on TV shows and movies. Waiting for pregnancy test results creates a natural narrative tension, and depictions of the home pregnancy test on screen became more and more common.

Since 1987, most advancements to the home pregnancy test have been relatively minor. As a walk down the pregnancy test aisle will demonstrate, the various brands like to compete for which can give results the earliest—with some promising an accurate result six days before a missed period. In 2003, Clearblue put out the digital home pregnancy test, which replaced the sometimes ambiguous line system with the words "pregnant" or "not pregnant." (While the digital tests have a computer chip to show the printed words, the technology behind detecting pregnancy in these tests is exactly the same as in non-digital tests, and still relies on hCG.)

The most interesting advancements in-home pregnancy testing have tried to address the limitations of the current test. In 2021, a small, women-owned company named Lia started selling the first flushable pregnancy test. Like the wand pregnancy tests, Lia users pee on one end of the stick, wait a couple of minutes to read their results—two lines mean you're pregnant—and then, because the product is made of biodegradable cellulose paper, it can be flushed down the toilet. For people who don't want others in their household to know they're pregnant (or even that they're worried about being pregnant), Lia offers the most discreet way to test for pregnancy. It leaves no trace of the result.

Gynuity, a nonprofit organization that supports women's reproductive health in the developing world, has helped develop a multi-level pregnancy test for women who travel long distances to obtain abortion pills and then can't return to the health clinic to ensure the medical abortion has worked. Clinics supported by Gynuity give women seeking abortion pills two of these multi-level tests, and each test has five windows (instead of the usual one) that are labeled with the amount of hCG each window tests for, with a range from 25 mlU/ml to 10,000 mlU/ml. Users are instructed to record the results of this first test: did every window show a dark second line or just some of the windows? (The test shows the level of pregnancy hormone in someone's body.) After the test, the abortion pills are taken, and then a week later the second test should be administered. If fewer windows show a second line in this second test, then that means the abortion was successful because hCG levels have gone down. This home pregnancy test allows for easier follow up after a medical abortion to ensure that the abortion pills worked as they should and eliminates—in most cases—the need for patients to travel to health clinics again.[17] While Gynuity has focused on reproductive care in the developing world, with the US Supreme Court overturning *Roe v. Wade*, which will outlaw or limit abortion access in more than half of American states, there may be a real need for the multi-level pregnancy test in the US as more people travel out of state for their abortions because they can't seek abortion care—or even follow-up care—in their home states.

Another home pregnancy test that's still in the works is one that can be read by blind or low-vision people without the help of another person or the use of a phone app. (The app allows blind and low-vision people to connect to someone who could read the test results for them.) This in-progress test, which was created by the Royal National Institute of Blind People and designed by Josh Wasserman, uses the same underlying biotechnology to detect hCG.[18] However, it's larger in size than conventional tests with a bigger absorbent pad at the tip for people who can't see where to aim their urine stream. It also uses tactile bumps to convey results, and the top of the test is brightly colored in yellow and pink to make it easier for people with low vision to distinguish the two sides. If a woman is pregnant, she will feel a set of bumps raised on the top of the test. Ultimately, this test allows blind and low-vision people to learn about their results in private, if that's what they wish, and without the help of someone who might be judgmental about the results.

The home pregnancy test of the twenty-first century has come a long way. But that doesn't mean it's a perfect technology. The home pregnancy test is ultimately a product of giant pharmaceutical companies and a capitalist market. The intent was always to sell more. Part 2 of this book will address the implications of the corporate culture of pregnancy testing and how that's come to influence the ways in which we understand pregnancy diagnosis itself.

PART 2

CULTURE

5 TELL ME DOCTOR

It's 1950 and a woman comes in to see her gynecologist because she suspects she might be pregnant. He asks about her symptoms: how many periods has she missed? Is she urinating more frequently? What about the size of her breasts? Oh, they're bigger? "Suppose you let me see them . . . Ah, yes, I imagine they are larger than when I examined you last." He tells her he notices that her nipples seem a bit darker as well. He pinches her areola until a tiny bit of colostrum escapes; another possible sign of pregnancy, he explains. Then he asks her to lie down, slips his fingers inside her and tells her that her cervix feels soft, like the lips on her mouth, which is another sign of pregnancy. Her vaginal canal looks purple, as opposed to its normal pinkish color, he finally notes. "Personally, I am entirely satisfied that you are pregnant," he concludes, adding that these are just presumptive signs of pregnancy. If she really wants to be sure, she'd need to take a rabbit test. The doctor's insistence that only a pregnancy test can confirm a pregnancy marked a new era in the history of pregnancy diagnosis.

This exchange was published in the *Ladies' Home Journal,* which ran a column called "Tell Me Doctor" for more than a decade.[1] While the column might sound like fiction—the doctor who penned this column refers to himself in the third person throughout the narrative—its stated intent was to educate women about their reproductive health and offer advice about various medical issues women might encounter. Still, each column reads like a short story with the doctor-author serving as the chapter's hero. After subjecting his patient to the intimate exam described above, Dr. Safford goes on to explain to her the latest in pregnancy tests: there's the outdated mouse test that's now been replaced by the rabbit test, which is easier to administer because the animal is bigger. There's also the African toad test, the doctor adds, which doesn't require killing an animal. His patient likes this idea because the thought of killing a rabbit unsettles her. However, the doctor tells her she doesn't have a choice in the matter. The toads are too hard to get and maintain, so if she wants a pregnancy test it will have to be with a rabbit. With that they agree that she'll come in the next morning with a cup of urine in a clean bottle, preferably a new one so that the urine isn't contaminated.

This 1950 column about pregnancy testing was the second "Tell Me Doctor" column in the magazine, which would go on to discuss topics like menstruation, childbirth, and abortion. No matter the subject, the intent of the column was supposedly to educate women about their reproductive health and their roles as mothers and wives. The doctor always knew best. In 1961, under a new doctor's authorship, the column would take up the pregnancy test again.[2] Whereas the patient in 1950 was excited about her possible pregnancy, Mrs. Welch, the pseudonymous patient in 1961, comes to see her doctor with more ambivalent feelings about her missed period. As she tells her doctor, she always seems to get pregnant at the most inopportune times. Mrs. Welch, the doctor sees in his files, has come to visit his clinic twice before: once twenty years ago, and the second time five years later. He's not her regular doctor because she lives at some distance. She travels for these visits because she doesn't want anyone in her town to suspect that she might be pregnant. Twenty years ago, when she asked for a pregnancy test, she was given the Aschheim-Zondek, or the mouse test. She had to wait for at least two weeks after her missed period before the test could be administered, and the positive result took yet another two weeks to obtain. When she came in five years later, the Friedman rabbit test would have been available, but the doctor refused to give her the test because he could tell she wanted to have an abortion. Instead, he ushered her out of his office and told her to talk to her husband about the problems in their marriage.

Now, fifteen years later, she's back again because she has missed several periods, and the thought of pregnancy at the age of forty-five—with her two children almost grown up and her husband's business floundering—worries her. She asks the doctor whether he could give her some pills that her friend told her were "the very latest thing in pregnancy tests."

They caused her friend to get her period back. Implicit in her request is the hope that maybe these pills might cause her to miscarry if she is indeed pregnant. The doctor crushes her hope, and tells her she's mistaken: these pills won't cause her period to return if she's pregnant. She'll only bleed if she's not. He follows with some chiding words: "twice now you've underrated your husband's love and understanding and maturity. It could be that a new offspring would give him a fresh interest and goal in life." The doctor once again decides against giving her a pregnancy test.

Many representations of pregnancy testing from the 1940s to the late 1980s, when women gradually stopped going to doctor's offices for a preliminary pregnancy diagnosis, involve a similar exchange. Like Mrs. Welch, women who visited their doctor for a test often assumed that nothing about their experience would be private. In a short story from 1967, published in *Redbook*, the protagonist has a pregnancy test at her local hospital and soon all her friends know it's positive because the husband of one friend works at the hospital.[3] In another story, also in *Redbook*, from 1949, the husband insists on coming with his wife when she makes an appointment for a pregnancy test with her doctor. Because he has some ambivalence about having another baby, he wants to talk to her doctor without her presence. After the exam, the two men step into the doctor's office to discuss his wife's possible diagnosis, and when the doctor refers to the potential second child as a son, the husband finds himself so moved that he decides his wife must keep the pregnancy.

Before she has a chance to talk to the doctor herself, the two men have decided her fate and the fate of her pregnancy.[4]

In 1969, in a *Cosmopolitan* article about the changing relationship between mothers and daughters, a young woman asks her mother how a friend could get a urine pregnancy test without visiting her doctor.[5] Twenty years later, the actress Susan Dey recalls in an interview for *Redbook* how when she was pregnant in 1977, she called the lab that was testing her urine for pregnancy because she wanted to know her results directly. The lab told her they could only release her results to her doctor.[6] This paternalistic culture of medicine ensured that doctors—who were most often men—controlled the narrative around women's pregnancy testing. It was difficult—if not impossible—to confirm a pregnancy without a doctor's help before 1978, and before the legalization of abortion some doctors even refused to provide a pregnancy test if they believed a woman was asking for one without the intention of having a baby. American doctors had tight control over access to pregnancy testing, especially as it became expected that pregnancy would be confirmed through a laboratory pregnancy test.

In many ways, women had little control over reproductive knowledge in this era, but there's one perspective that's shared even less often: that of someone responsible for the daily work of maintaining the animals required for these tests. Richard Wright's 1945 memoir *Black Boy* has one of the few representations of the other side of pregnancy testing.[7] In the 1930s, Wright started working for a laboratory in the basement of a major Chicago hospital that served mostly white people. He was naturally curious about the animals he fed and whose cages he cleaned, so he asked a doctor about how the pregnancy tests worked. He was summarily dismissed as not being smart enough to understand because he was Black and worked a menial job. Later, however, Wright demonstrates how critical his role was in the outcome of these tests. Two other laboratory workers, both Black men, got into an argument that turned physical, and in their anger they accidentally knocked over the cages that housed the rabbits and various other animals used in the doctors' tests and experiments. Many of the animals escaped or were crushed by the commotion. Quickly, Wright and his co-workers realized that this mess would cost them their jobs: they righted the cages and as best as possible restored the animals to their places. In some cases, it was impossible to match the rabbits to the correct cages, and in others the animal was gone. So they grabbed some animals that hadn't been tested yet and stuck them into random cages. Wright was never told how the tests worked, but in that moment, he recognized that he had just skewed the results for the doctors—and their patients waiting to hear about their pregnancy tests.

As Wright understood, the pregnancy test had paternalistic power—power that he unintentionally undermined—because it allowed doctors to know about the inner workings of women's bodies before them. The test gave doctors a god-like power; it became a way to definitively diagnose pregnancy and therefore define when a pregnancy began. However, underlying that power was both an abuse of animals and the workers—Black workers in this case—who did the daily work of tending to these animals. Wright considered telling his supervisor—the doctor—about the accident, but he knew it would mean the loss of his job and the jobs of his co-workers. His boss didn't view him as a human being but as "close kin to the animals [they] tended." He was just an instrument, like the animals, in a white, male-dominated culture that gave doctors the knowledge and power to exert control over people not like them. The pregnancy test was just one tool among many that was used to shape the narrative of people's lives, and as long as it relied on doctors to impart information that people desperately wanted, it would give doctors an outsized influence over the course of those lives. People would have to *ask*—sometimes even plead—for that knowledge. While the home pregnancy test might have subverted some of this power, in other ways, it just shifted authority from the direct hands of doctors to a more consumerist model of attaining knowledge.[8]

6 THE PSYCHOLOGI-CAL TORTURE OF A BEAUTIFUL YOUNG WOMAN

In 1997, Clearblue released a provocative fifteen-second black-and-white commercial that emphasized the anxiety inherent in pregnancy testing. An image of a ticking clock fills the screen, and we hear the seconds go by as a female narrator tells us, "When you're waiting to find out if you're pregnant or not, nothing else in the world matters." The numbers on the clock's face are replaced with the words "Yes" and "No" in alternating repeating order: the two possible answers for a pregnancy test.[1] The commercial has a topsy-turvy effect on viewers, and it captures well the focus women feel when they take a pregnancy test. Nothing else matters in the minute it takes to read the results of your test. While it may surprise people to learn that David Lynch, best known for directing the popular TV series *Twin Peaks*, directed this commercial for a pregnancy test, the commercial itself feels like a Lynch production in all its disorienting effects.

In a *New York Times* article, Lynch told his interviewer that he immediately jumped on the opportunity to advertise the pregnancy test. At first he said it was because he "liked the bold, simple concept," but a copywriter who worked closely with him on the project corrected him: "Mr. Lynch," she said, "you were attracted to this because it involves the psychological torture of a beautiful young woman." He acknowledged that this was true, and shared that at the time of shooting he asked a pregnant woman on set to take a pregnancy test so he could swap it with the one he asked the actress to take. He wanted to film her reaction when she saw the test was unexpectedly positive. He was eager to psychologically torture this beautiful young woman. While the actress didn't give away her shock on camera, as soon as the cameras stopped rolling, she screamed, "You bastard! Very funny."[2]

Lynch's commercial for the pregnancy test was unusual at the time because almost all other commercials until then had been pitched to women who wanted to be pregnant. In contrast, Lynch's commercial left the emotional response to the test ambiguous. His commercial ends with a beautiful, young, white woman's face on screen looking at her test nervously. When the minute has passed, her face breaks into a smile. She's clearly pleased with the test and its message, but we don't learn why exactly. Is it positive or negative? Instead, the commercial tries to capture a mood the pregnancy test so often evokes: the desire to know as soon as possible, and the suspense inherent in that desire. Clearblue was offering potential customers results in just one minute, which was quicker than any other test on the market at that point. By 1997, when the commercial aired, the pregnancy test was well on its way to becoming the popular object we know today. It was already changing our relationship to pregnancy, and it would continue to transform our relationship to our reproductive bodies.

Advertising the Home Pregnancy Test

Many of the earliest aired home pregnancy test commercials from the late 1980s and early 1990s starred men, which was a way of pitching the advertisements to married or coupled women. One common trope portrayed women using the test to tell their husbands about their pregnancy, always to a happy response.[3] Another e.p.t. commercial from 1990 only shows male actors as they presumably receive the news about their partner's positive test. All of them are pleased with the news, but they express this joy with a range of shocked, wordless, and bumbling responses. The new e.p.t. pregnancy test, the commercial's female narrator tells viewers, is "a faster, easier way to get the big news."[4] Implicit in this voiceover is that they're receiving this news from their wives, and that it will be good news if the test is positive.

Another e.p.t. commercial from 1986 shows a man blocking access to a public phone because he's waiting for his wife to call with the news about her home pregnancy test. The test results would take ten minutes, and by the time the countdown has reached two minutes, a small crowd of people waiting to use the phone has formed around him. When the phone finally rings, we don't hear the news, but he's clearly hoping it's positive.[5] Other commercials from the early 1990s, if they don't feature men, emphasize their brand's easier way to obtain results, either because urine no longer needed to be collected in a cup for the dipstick test or because their test was easier to use or read.[6] No matter what each of these commercials emphasized, they all framed the pregnancy announcement as an event—one between a man, a woman, and this purchased object.

In 1994, e.p.t. started using people who weren't actors in their commercials to show real couples waiting to get their result on screen. They also diversified who appeared on screen and featured Black couples and interracial couples who had just taken the test. In one commercial, a Black couple discusses their eagerness to have a child. When someone off-screen hands the woman her test, she joyfully tells her husband, "We're pregnant." They embrace, and the husband tells the camera, "See, I kind of thought she was," as he touches her stomach.[7] In another version of this commercial, a white couple is shown discussing why they're taking a pregnancy test. The woman tells the camera, "My body tells me I might be, but then, you know, a woman's body is kind of—you never know." When her husband adds that they're at a good age to have children, and he's ready, she interjects, "I've always been ready." When someone off-camera hands her the test, she looks at it almost in disbelief, "It's negative," she tells her husband. "Don't get worried," he tells her as he rubs her shoulders. Her disappointment is evident as her eyes water, holding back tears. The commercial ends with her husband saying, "We're going to keep trying."[8]

While each of these commercials has a different ending, they both emphasize the natural dramatic tension of the pregnancy test as a singular moment that unites the couple. They create a story of how a pregnancy (or non-pregnancy) diagnosis should be shared, while giving the home pregnancy test the starring role. In both stories, at least one person in the couple suspected pregnancy, but that suspicion wasn't always right. Only the home pregnancy test could confirm the woman's ontological state, giving the test a supreme importance in their reproductive lives.

Six Days Before a Missed Period

More recently, home pregnancy tests have played a large role in creating community in online infertility forums. These forums have popularized the phrase "the two-week wait," which is the recommended waiting time from either ovulation or from an intrauterine insemination (IUI) or in-vitro fertilization (IVF) procedure in a clinic. The two-week wait refers to the approximate time it takes for a blastocyst to form, implant in the uterus, and begin producing enough hCG for a pregnancy test to measure. Because some pregnancy tests can (more unreliably) detect early pregnancy six days before a missed period, there are people who choose to test for pregnancy only eight days after ovulation or insemination. On *The Bump*, an online forum for all things pregnancy, the thread with the most comments and views is titled, "What Does a Positive Pregnancy Test Really Look Like??" [*sic*]. It has 1,725 replies and 695,283 views.[9] The first message on this forum, posted by BumpJackie, is dated January 2014 and invites readers to share their pregnancy test results:

> Pregnancy tests can be tough to decipher—pregnant, not pregnant . . . that kinda looks like a line? What does a positive pregnancy test *reaaaaaly* look like? [*sic*] Help others figure out what their test says:
>
> How did you know yours truly was positive? What brand did you use? Share a picture of it here or email it to photos @thebump.com

In response, women share hundreds of pregnancy test images, recommend their favorite brands, and discuss what a second faint line might mean. In almost all these forums, a shared language has emerged around pregnancy testing.

The First Response/Early Response tests are often shortened to FRER, and the date of testing is abbreviated to indicate how many days after ovulation a test was taken; 8DPO, for example, means eight days post-ovulation. Some women post multiple tests showing the progression of the second line getting darker with each passing day. As madfam0405 explained on the forum, she took so many tests because she was "a bit paranoid after two chemicals!" Some women post photos of their tests and ask other forum participants whether the faint second line could mean they're pregnant. Others post positive pregnancy tests to ask whether they should be concerned because the second line isn't getting darker.

One woman shared her positive pregnancy tests with the note, "Sadly the happiness of these have ended with bad news as I have suffered a blighted ovum. Still confused how your body can think it is pregnant without a baby." A blighted ovum is when an early embryo stops developing but an empty gestational sac is still present. Because the placenta still grows until a miscarriage occurs, and because the placenta rather than the embryo produces hCG, levels will rise and lead to a positive pregnancy test. As Bizliz35, who also posted about her blighted ovum, learned, a pregnancy test doesn't actually test for whether a viable pregnancy is present. It simply tests whether hCG is being produced. These forums have become a way for women to give each other support and better understand a technology that is marketed as simple and easy to understand, but in fact, can be interpreted in multiple ways, especially when the results are ambiguous.

Since its introduction to the American public, the home pregnancy test has been heavily marketed to obscure that ambiguity. My local drugstore in Queens, New York carries several brands, and each one emphasizes a different way of knowing results sooner, more accurately, or more clearly. First Response, one of the leading American brands, stresses that results can be known in one minute and are 99 percent accurate. The digital version of First Response, which both shows one or two lines and the digital words "Yes +" or "No -," boasts that the test can give results as soon as six days before a missed period. Then in smaller words on the packaging, the manufacturer notes that the test is only 99 percent accurate "on the day of your missed period." Clearblue similarly advertises in large type that the test "Can Tell You 6 Days Sooner Than Your Missed Period," with the caveat in smaller print that it's only over 99 percent accurate from the day of your first missed period.

What happens inside a body six days before a pregnancy that can be detected? Pregnancy technically begins when a fertilized egg implants into the uterus, which can take three to four days after fertilization. The entire process from fertilization to implantation is not consistent and can take as few as eight days and as many as twelve days. Half of all fertilized eggs pass through the uterus during menstruation, either only partially implanting or not implanting at all. Therefore, six days before a period begins, a woman could have a blastocyst that has implanted and started the process of becoming an embryo or she could have a fertilized egg still in the process of almost implanting. In the former case, the ovaries start producing hCG only after implantation, and a home pregnancy test would be positive. In the latter case, the pregnancy test would not detect hCG and the test would be negative, even if implantation occurs the next day.

Given these various scenarios, a negative pregnancy test result could be wrong because the test was taken too early, despite the optimistic promises advertised on the box, and a positive result could be wrong because it detects a very early pregnancy that doesn't develop, otherwise known as a chemical, or biochemical, pregnancy. In this case, usually because of genetic abnormalities, a blastocyst begins implanting but then quickly stops. Menstruation usually isn't delayed, and someone might only experience a slightly heavier period that cycle. Some studies suggest that between eight percent and thirty-three percent of pregnancies end this way.[10]

Is it accurate, then, to even call them pregnancies? Before the invention of the incredibly sensitive home pregnancy test, there would have been no way of knowing that a blastocyst had been formed that failed to fully implant to continue a pregnancy. The home pregnancy test created this new category of pregnancy, which primarily impacts women who are anxious to be pregnant. (Why else would you take a test six days before your missed period?) There's another way of looking at a chemical pregnancy: Did a miscarriage happen if you didn't know you were pregnant to begin with?[11] The majority of home pregnancy tests claim to be over 99 percent accurate, despite the uncertain status of very early pregnancies. Contrary to Lynch's commercial that suggests a pregnancy test can give only a yes or no answer, it turns out you can be ambiguously pregnant.

While the most popular name brand pregnancy tests like First Response and Clearblue can cost between $15 and $25—not cheap, especially if you're planning to take multiple tests—dollar stores, some drugstores, and online vendors now sell dollar tests that contain a bundle of tests, sometimes more than ten in a package. These tests use the same technology as the more expensive brands, and the FDA reports that they are just as accurate, although might not be as sensitive, which means they shouldn't be taken before a missed period.[12] Still, these dollar tests have allowed home pregnancy tests to become more accessible than ever before, and women who are eager or anxious about getting pregnant often use several in a cycle. However, it's also resulted in women testing earlier and earlier in their cycles, when results are more likely to be ambiguous or lead to heartbreaking conclusions. There's a good reason the marketing for the pregnancy test plays on women's desires to know whether or not they're pregnant. But for some women, it has turned the pregnancy test into an object of obsession, perhaps even an instrument of psychological torture. And in doing so, it's manipulated our very understanding of when pregnancy begins and what it means in those early, uncertain days of embryo formation.

7 THERE IS NO PREGNANCY WITHOUT THE PREGNANCY TEST

The advent of home pregnancy testing shifted the drama of waiting for a test result into women's hands. It became an individualized, private experience—one that could be purchased. Perhaps then, it's no surprise that by the late 1980s, the pregnancy test began to regularly appear on TV shows to announce pregnancy. Pregnancy announcements make for exciting TV. In 1988, the popular soap operas *Guiding Light* and *As the World Turns* both showed characters taking a pregnancy test. There's of course Murphy Brown's pregnancy test in 1991, discussed earlier. The 2007 movie *Knocked Up* reenacts this scene—and stresses not only the test's dramatic value but its comedic resonances, too—when the film's protagonist also buys more than a dozen tests to confirm her pregnancy. It's not an exaggeration to say that on TV and film today there is no pregnancy without the home pregnancy test. The home pregnancy test has become so ubiquitous that even someone who has never used one can easily identify it.

I Love Lucy was the first TV show to announce a pregnancy on air, and since then television producers learned that there's rarely a better way to boost ratings than when a character becomes pregnant. With the invention of the home pregnancy test, audiences could watch in real time as characters learned about their pregnancies. The home pregnancy test created a window into an intimate moment that most of us are never privy to it unless it happens to us. At the same time, TV shows could now tell us earlier than ever when a character is pregnant, and therefore employ a pregnancy-related storyline over even more episodes. In the hands of television show producers, the home pregnancy test is a capitalist tool, a product for entertainment.

In the twenty-first century, social media has given the pregnancy test even more prominence. Perhaps one measure of the pregnancy test's ubiquity is on the popular app TikTok where users post short videos. In 2020, a "pregnancy test filter" was released that supposedly (but not really) determines whether a user is pregnant. Users on the site created dramatic videos that featured the filter on screen, which looks like a wand pregnancy test, as viewers watched and waited to see what the pregnancy test told the user.[1] The filter plays on the excitement—and adrenaline rush—of taking a pregnancy test.

More seriously, on Instagram, #pregnancytest and its variations brings up thousands of posts showing users sharing their pregnancy test results with the public. Most show the results of a positive pregnancy test with the familiar two lines. A few show a progression of pregnancy tests with the second line darkening with each passing day as the amount of hCG doubles in their urine. Some women openly discuss their struggles with infertility on Instagram, and the positive pregnancy test is presented as the realization of a long-awaited moment. Other women share that they recognize a positive pregnancy test doesn't mean they'll have a baby in eight months. Fewer women share negative tests, but those can be found on Instagram too, especially on accounts created for sharing experiences with assisted reproductive technologies like IVF. While there are dozens of articles on the internet advising women not to share their pee-soaked tests on social media because it's not "classy," or because it's too private or because it's too early to announce a pregnancy given the risk of miscarriage, influencers and celebrities are often paid by the biggest pregnancy test companies to promote their brand and have now normalized posting images of home pregnancy test results.[2] As one article in the *New York Times* about this culture is subtitled, "Content Begins at Conception."[3] And what better way to announce conception than the pregnancy test. In the twenty-first century, it's hard to imagine a pregnancy that doesn't begin with it.

Like a Scene from a Romantic Comedy

Like the *Mona Lisa*, the pregnancy test is now recognizable everywhere, replicated many times over, but still an important signifier of a major event. It's been in turn comedic and commercial. Yet, no matter how many times we might have seen or taken a pregnancy test, it still carries an emotional weight. Emily Rapp Black's 2021 memoir *Sanctuary* about pregnancy and parenting after the death of her first child is a testament to the test's significance.[4] Black begins the fifth chapter of *Sanctuary* with a narrative about pregnancy testing that's likely familiar to any person desperate to be pregnant. She has woken up before dawn, likely waiting to test for pregnancy with urine after a night of sleep, which is what all home pregnancy tests recommend if you're to get early results. Even before her partner wakes, she has taken four tests, all positive. After the fourth result confirms the three before it, she wakes up her partner and hands him the test while joking, "This is like a scene from a romantic comedy."

Except it's not. It's a scene from the life of a woman who has tragically lost her first child; divorced the father of that child; and in her early forties, after some fertility treatment, hopes she can get pregnant again. The positive pregnancy test carries all that emotional baggage and more. The pregnancy test might have the veneer of comedy, but underneath is the seriousness of life and death. As she sits alone in her bathroom, in those minutes as she waits for the first and then hopefully second line to appear, she remembers how from the moment her son was diagnosed with Tay-Sachs, the fatal disease that would kill him, she wanted another child. Everything hangs on this test. There's nothing funny about it at all as her trembling hands reveal the gravity of the situation for her.

Black visits her doctor because until he confirms her pregnancy, those four positive tests feel like an illusion that could evaporate. And in fact, when he gives her a sonogram, he dismissively tells her that the pregnancy is a "no-go" because no heartbeat can be found. Black is devastated. Her friend Elizabeth had reassuringly told her, "I'm sure you're preggo. Those things are super accurate." They're super accurate, except they can't tell you when a pregnancy isn't viable. The derisive doctor, who never asks for her name, who tells her she "must be Jewish" (she isn't) because she carries the gene for Tay-Sachs, and who shows her no compassion when he reports that all he sees is a fetal pole with no heartbeat, ends up being wrong too. A week later when Black returns to the fertility clinic with her partner, a kinder doctor happily reports the "nice and strong" heartbeat. Eight months later Black gives birth to her daughter. Doctors, like pregnancy tests, are not infallible, and sometimes when you take a pregnancy test too early the timeline of your pregnancy can be skewed, too.

Or take another show that focuses on the drama of infertility: Aziz Ansari's *Master of None*, whose third season is titled *Moments in Love*, directs its attention to the relationship between Denise and Alicia. The season, which premiered in Spring 2021, gained attention for its intimate depiction of a Black lesbian woman's struggle to get pregnant on her own.[5] In the first episode of the season, Alicia convinces Denise to try artificial insemination at home with the help of a friend's sperm. Amazingly, at first, everything goes to plan: their friend quickly agrees to be the donor; Denise is able to inseminate Alicia at home in a scene that manages to be both romantic and technical; and then the show fast forwards through the two-week wait, that dreaded time it takes before a home pregnancy test can accurately depict results. We see Alicia sitting on the edge of the tub with a wand pregnancy test in her hand, tapping it nervously during the minute it takes to show its results. Then she looks at it in disbelief—it's positive. The scene demonstrates the visual power of the home pregnancy test. The entire exchange is wordless, but the home pregnancy test is now so familiar that no viewer watching this scene will wonder why Alicia and Denise hug each other in joy after spending sixty seconds looking at a white stick. The last ten minutes of the episode, from the moment Alicia reads her pregnancy test, have very few words. Ansari only shows us Alicia's joy and then her loss when she has a miscarriage. While her pregnancy test was certainly accurate, the episode is as good an example as any for how a positive result does not always end with a baby.

The pregnancy test has become the emotional signifier of pregnancy. As Black implies in her memoir, it's almost clichéd, comedic. Every time we might use a pregnancy test, we can recall a character in a movie, TV show, or novel using one as well. For some people, taking a pregnancy test might even feel like a rite of passage, whether they hope for a positive or negative result. The experience of taking the test has become so ubiquitous that it's soundless. It's an expected ritual in our reproductive lives.

8 THE SCIENCE FICTION OF PREGNANCY TESTING

When Margaret Atwood published *The Handmaid's Tale* in 1985 the home pregnancy test would have been well stocked in American drugstores, if reluctantly embraced. Certainly, in the fictional dystopian Gilead of the novel, the world where women's rights—and especially their reproductive rights—have been stripped away, any remaining home pregnancy tests would have been thrown in the pyre with the banned books or put under lock and key in doctors' offices. However, in the twenty-first-century TV retelling of *The Handmaid's Tale*, a home pregnancy test does survive. In the last episode of the first season, which premiered in 2017, Serena Joy, the infertile wife of a powerful commander, angrily bursts into June's room after she discovers that her husband has been cavorting with the handmaid outside of their regularly scheduled and compulsory sexual encounters. In this oppressive world, fertile women like June have been forced to serve as reproductive surrogates for powerful, childless couples like Serena Joy and her husband, Commander Waterford.

According to the rules of this dystopia, June's sexual encounters with Waterford are supposed to be ritualized and scheduled, with Serena always present. If a child is conceived it will be Serena's by law. So when Serena discovers that her husband has violated this norm, and has presumably had sex with June without her presence, she accosts June with a pregnancy test, presumably one that she purchased on the black market. The scene upends everything about how the home pregnancy test has been marketed. Whereas the home pregnancy test was supposed to help women feel in control of their reproductive lives and ensure privacy when women learned whether they were pregnant (or not), here Serena thrusts a test at June while demanding she sit on the toilet. When June tells her she can't urinate on demand, Serena patronizes her and tells her not to be a child. She watches June's every move, and we watch with her as the slow, intimate sound of June's urine trickles into the toilet, presumably landing on the pregnancy test's absorbent tip on the way. As soon as June is done, Serena snatches the wand away to wait for the results in the next room. June won't know the results of the test until Serena chooses to share them. The audience won't either. The show has us wait for the full minute, as we watch June bent over the bathtub, bleeding into its smooth, white porcelain surface from Serena's beating, while Serena kneels on the floor of the bedroom in a praying position.

The image of Serena anxiously hunched over the pregnancy test wand might feel relatable to any woman who has purchased her test hoping for a positive result. For Serena, the test's answer represents the hope that she might finally be healed of her many years of unwanted childlessness. Yet, we also know that Serena is using the home pregnancy test as a weapon. When she steps back into the bathroom she shows June the pregnancy test, and the audience sees its result at the same time as June. There's a blue plus sign. June is pregnant. Serena is overjoyed; June is devastated.

The pregnancy test didn't start appearing in reproductive dystopias until the late twentieth century, but these days it's everywhere. In Alaya Dawn Johnson's science fictional short story, "They Shall Salt the Earth with Seeds of Glass," a Black community has been colonized by the mysterious glassmen, who never directly appear to them but control their movements through robots made of glass.[1] The community lives on the edge of death because of regular bombings that destroy their fields, and sometimes their families as well. Libby, the story's narrator, learns in the opening passages that her sister is pregnant when she hands her the results of her pregnancy test. This kit is science fictional, and although it's no bigger than a hand, it has a gauge that tells its user how far along she is in the pregnancy. On the far left is "Not Pregnant" and on the far right is "Nine Months." Lines mark the eight months in between. An inscription in large letters warns users, "All fetuses are to be carried to full term." While the glassmen don't provide medical supplies for the burns people endure from the regular bombings, they will hand out a pregnancy test whenever it's requested. This test isn't meant to give people control over their reproductive lives— it's meant to collect knowledge to ensure no one sneaks off to have an abortion.

In the epilogue to Atwood's novel, which takes place in 2195 at a conference dedicated to the discovery of the handmaid's journals, Professor Pieixoto offhandedly mentions Romania's practice of compulsory pregnancy tests for women in the 1980s.[2] This reference is not science fiction but was in fact part of a Romanian plan to promote population growth starting in 1967. Abortion at this point was deemed illegal, and all women of childbearing age were required to have regular gynecological exams at work, including pregnancy testing. The Romanian state wasn't shy about explaining that this surveillance was intended to monitor women in case they planned to have an abortion. (The 2007 Romanian film *4 Months, 3 Weeks and 2 Days* portrays this political moment.)

A compulsory pregnancy test might sound not only dystopian but also foreign to many Americans living in the twenty-first century. Yet, until 2020, women soldiers in the National Guard had to take pregnancy tests every three months if they wanted to keep their jobs. One former soldier recalls how because she refused to sign the consent form for the compulsory tests—rightly arguing that this was an invasion of her privacy—she was fired.[3] As late as 1988, homeless women in New York City were required to have a pregnancy test if they wanted housing from the city. A *Los Angeles Times* article describes a scene in an NYC homeless shelter that could be taken out of a page in a dystopian novel: homeless women in waiting rooms stripping down their babies on stained bare mattresses to prepare for examinations, while taking turns going to the bathroom where a nurse is waiting to give them a pregnancy test. The results, which the nurse saw first, determined what kind of room they would get, if they would get one at all in New York City's overcrowded, dirty, and pest-infested shelter system. [4]

In 2013, the American Civil Liberties Union filed a lawsuit against Alameda County Jails for forcing all women—regardless of age—to take a pregnancy test after their arrest. One woman described how shortly after her arrest a guard refused to give her a menstrual pad and instead insisted she take a pregnancy test.[5] In other words, the science fictional examples of the pregnancy test's ability to be used as a tool of coercion are not science fictional at all. In fact, when it comes to the state's desire to control our reproductive lives, sometimes the world we live in is as dystopian—if not more so—than what's represented in fiction. Leni Zumas's novel *Red Clocks* is yet another example.

Border Crossings

In *Red Clocks* abortion has been outlawed in the United States from the moment of conception.[6] A new president, with the support of Congress, passes a law that gives "personhood" to embryos. Women who seek an abortion, even if they never go through with it, can be charged with conspiring to murder; anyone who provides an abortion is similarly prosecuted. Because this fictional US Government foresaw that women would cross the northern border to have legal abortions in Canada, the two countries agree that any woman of childbearing age who is suspected of coming into Canada to have an abortion can be stopped, questioned, and arrested. She can also be forced to take a pregnancy test. In one scene, a fifteen-year-old girl is told to pee in a cup for a pregnancy test. Refusing to do so can also lead to arrest.

While Zumas's dystopian novel might be science fictional, forcing women to take pregnancy tests at national borders is not. In August 1996, the US Government found that Mexican women looking for employment at export-processing factories, or *maquiladoras*, were forced to take a pregnancy test as a condition of hiring. Because these jobs paid significantly more than other Mexican jobs, most women were reluctant to challenge these policies and submitted to the tests, which required them to hand over a cup of urine that would then be tested by a nurse. If a woman was found pregnant, she was not hired.[7] As recently as 2018, the Fair Labor Association, an NGO that works to improve migrant workers' lives, reported that migrant women going to work in Malaysia were regularly subjected to pregnancy tests as a border crossing requirement since the government knew they were coming to seek work. They were also routinely given pregnancy tests as a condition of continued employment.[8]

Coercive pregnancy testing for women applying for jobs has an even longer history on the northern side of the American border. In the 1970s, soon after the laboratory pregnancy tests became the new standard for pregnancy diagnosis, it wasn't uncommon for large companies to secretly give women a pregnancy test before hiring them. In July 1970, several newspapers reported that the Chesapeake and Potomac Telephone Co. based in DC asked all women who applied for a job for a urine sample that was then tested for pregnancy without their consent. The company medical director admitted that this was his idea after he observed that women who have children rarely come back to their positions after having a child.[9] His rationale for administering these tests without consent was that the company didn't want to waste money training women if they were to leave just a few months later to have a baby. In 1987, a similar story broke, but this time it was reported that women recruited to the Philadelphia police force had been routinely given secret pregnancy tests for the last two years.[10] While the women had been told their urine would be tested for drugs when they applied, they were not told about the pregnancy tests.

More recently, in 2019, *Fox News* reported that US Immigration and Customs Enforcement, or ICE, gives all migrant girls and women over the age of ten a pregnancy test when they cross the border and arrive at a detention center.[11] The reporting frames this testing as beneficial to the girls and women subjected to these tests because of the dangers inherent in the perilous journey. However, the report omits to mention whether these tests are consensual and whether girls and women who are found to be pregnant are given any kind of support.

Pregnancy Resource Centers

"A squat gray building in the middle of a strip mall" outside of town; a waiting area with Black girls who won't make eye contact with her; a white counselor who condescends to her, speaks to her with the voice of a kindergarten teacher and assumes she doesn't know about condoms and safe sex. Brit Bennett's novel *The Mothers* introduces this scene in its opening pages. Nadia, a young woman at the top of her class, is waiting for her period to arrive. After several weeks of its absence, she takes a bus to a free pregnancy test clinic and is treated like another girl too dumb to know that she should have used a condom. When she tells her boyfriend, his first response is, "Fuck." And then, "Are you sure?" and then again, "But are you *sure* sure?" Of course, she's sure.[12] She took a pregnancy test. They're never wrong. Bennett's novel isn't science fictional, but its depiction of pregnancy crisis centers reflects a trend in American reproductive health that feels scarier than some of the scariest representations of women's healthcare in science fiction.

The pregnancy crisis center Nadia visits doesn't coerce her to keep her pregnancy, but its depiction offers insight into why a young woman might choose to have a pregnancy test at such a clinic and the repercussions of that choice. Women like Nadia, who are low income, young, and Black are far more likely to go to a pregnancy resource center simply because they offer pregnancy tests for free. At the same time, many women also choose to go to a pregnancy resource center to confirm their pregnancies.[13] A study published in 2020 found that for some women having their tests confirmed by a clinic, even if they used home pregnancy tests, felt more official and real. In other cases, it helped them convince a family member or sexual partner that the pregnancy was real. Other women said that a positive pregnancy test by a clinic allowed them to go on Medicaid. While many women were initially attracted to these clinics because they offered a free pregnancy test, several appreciated the support they received after they decided to keep their pregnancies.

Yet, organizations like NARAL Pro-Choice America and the American Medical Association agree that pregnancy resource centers often use unethical tactics, like lying about the side effects of abortion, in order to manipulate the patients that come through their door.[14] They first attract patients by offering free services, often starting with the pregnancy test. For however affordable the home pregnancy test has become, it still costs something. That's money that could be used for food, rent, or childcare. These pregnancy resource centers are filling a need for low-income women without access to healthcare who also want to know whether they're pregnant as soon as possible. They don't get the privilege of learning this news in the privacy of their homes without someone judging their reaction.

In 2011, anthropologist Khiara Bridges published an ethnography of women of color's experience of pregnancy and prenatal care. For her study, Bridges volunteered at a women's health clinic that she calls Alpha. Primarily serving women of color and working-class women, the clinic, which Bridges describes at one point as "barely controlled bedlam," also serves as some women's only access to prenatal care. And yet, as Bridges notes, gaining access to that care is a convoluted process that begins with a pregnancy test. A woman who comes to Alpha seeking prenatal care must first take a pregnancy test at the center. If the test is positive, someone from the clinic calls her the next day and schedules an appointment with a social worker, nurse, nutritionist, and financial officer; only *after* she meets with them can she schedule an appointment with a doctor, midwife, or nurse practitioner to begin her prenatal care. This entire process sometimes takes weeks. One woman, who felt especially frustrated by the long wait, angrily told Bridges, "Your fucking system is stupid."[15]

In this case, the pregnancy test serves as a way to add a level of bureaucracy, and so it's not surprising some women would see it as simply another delay, especially if they entered the clinic for immediate care and already have pregnancy confirmation. Why do they have to wait yet another day to get their results, and why are the results not made known to them immediately? Why can't someone talk to them that same day and make them feel like they're taking an active role in their reproductive health? Wasn't that the promise of the pregnancy test? In many cases, the pregnancy resource center might offer pregnancy test results sooner and more cheaply than any other method available but with the hidden cost of anti-abortion rhetoric if the test is positive. Why can't the women's health clinic do the same?

The Pregnancy Test at the End of the World

The home pregnancy test has become so ubiquitous that even at the end of the world women seem to be able to find them. In Ling Ma's 2018 novel *Severance* about a global pandemic that decimates the world's population, the novel's protagonist goes looking for a pregnancy test after her period fails to come. She soon discovers that because of the pandemic, all major drugstores have closed, but in a still open Korean general store, she finds an "off-brand Korean pregnancy test" and purchases two. Although this test has instructions in Korean she can't read, the two lines that appear on the stick are universal enough that she knows what they mean. The next evening she takes the second test; the results are the same.[16] Louise Erdrich, who also imagines an apocalyptic world in her novel *Future Home of the Living God,* begins her novel with a pregnancy test. For Cedar, the narrator, the pregnancy test doesn't just tell her whether or not she's pregnant, it also tells her whether she should have an abortion. Cedar tells us that almost ten years prior, she took a pregnancy test and immediately upon seeing the positive result knew she would have an abortion. This time around, "the dipstick test filled me *yes.*"[17] For Cedar, having a baby as the world is falling apart is dangerous, and the "yes" of her test result is all she can hear.

The horror film *False Positive* released in 2021 begins with a negative pregnancy test, despite the title, but shortly after the main character's fertility treatment she learns of her positive pregnancy test from her doctor. The film makes literal what Ma and Erdrich's science fictional novels about pregnancy more subtly depict: the ways in which the medical establishment—and patriarchy—have a vested interest in controlling reproductive bodies. A positive pregnancy test, once publicly known, becomes a tool to expedite that process with the excuse that the pregnant body needs extra protection. In the film, Lucy's concerns about her pregnancy are dismissed, and she's treated as mentally unstable. After some snooping, she learns that information about her pregnancy has been intentionally withheld from her.[18] A pregnant body needs to be contained and controlled because it's a vessel for a future child; in both *Severance* and *Future Home* that happens quite literally. While the two narrators try to keep their pregnancies hidden for as long as possible, eventually men—

in whom they've confided—give them away. In *Severance,* the pregnant Candace is locked up in a store in a deserted mall by a man claiming it's for her own care. Cedar, the Native American protagonist of *Future Home,* is confined in a series of makeshift hospitals that really serve as prisons for pregnant women. As soon as her baby is born, he's taken away.

Some of the literary examples I've drawn on depict white women with relative means—at least before the apocalyptic events that decimate their worlds. However, almost all the real-world examples I've drawn on involve women of color, immigrant women, women with limited economic means, and disabled women. As Dorothy Roberts has argued, "the denial of Black reproductive autonomy serves the interests of white supremacy."[19] The reproductive technologies that have liberated women with privilege have served to oppress women without those privileges. The technology of the pregnancy test has been no exception.

The healthcare system and pharmaceutical companies in the mid-twentieth century created a culture that is now reflected in all forms of media, from magazine articles to short stories to social media; today there is no pregnancy without the pregnancy test. The wand test is such a commonplace object that it no longer needs an explanation. It took less than thirty years for the home pregnancy test as we know it to gain such legibility. But that doesn't mean a pregnancy diagnosis is always correct, simple, or without the mediating judgment of a paternalistic doctor. It also doesn't mean the pregnancy test can't do harm.

In some ways we've come a long way from the Dr. Saffords of the 1950s and 60s who had the authority to refuse to give their patients pregnancy tests and took husbands to their offices for man-to-man chats about their pregnant wives. And in other ways, perhaps we've come to rely too deeply on the home pregnancy test, and the alluring narrative of its packaging. There's little in this world that's 99 percent accurate.

AFTERWORD

In Spring 2022, I was contacted by a consulting team working on introducing a new kind of home pregnancy test to the market: this test would tell users not only whether they were pregnant but how far along they were in their pregnancy. I spoke to the team just a few months after Texas enacted SB 8, the state senate bill that declared abortion illegal in the state if performed after six weeks and that awarded vigilantes ten thousand dollars if they reported anyone who has or tries to have an abortion after six weeks. One of the many absurdities of this law is that often people don't find out that they're pregnant until they're past six weeks along. If you take a pregnancy test on the first day of a missed period, you would be four weeks pregnant. If you waited until your period was two weeks late—which some doctors advise because menstrual cycles are often irregular—you'd already be at six weeks. In theory, then, a new home pregnancy test that could date a pregnancy for you might be helpful.

Yet, as I told the two women on the consulting team, an accessible and easy-to-use pregnancy test that could date a pregnancy with precision cuts both ways. I opened this book with the story of my first experience using a home pregnancy test. My period was two weeks late when I took that first home pregnancy test, and when I arrived at Planned Parenthood and received a sonogram I was told I was more than six weeks pregnant. I didn't have an abortion at that very moment: I made an appointment to come back the following week because I needed someone pick me up from the clinic after the procedure. Under Texas's SB 8 law I would have already missed my chance for an abortion.

While a home pregnancy test that dates a pregnancy might be helpful for people who want to be pregnant—or have struggled with infertility—the stories in this book suggest how such a test could be used to criminalize people seeking abortions and abortion providers. Creating a tool that could measure a pregnancy with precision might be used not only to turn away people seeking abortions, but also as evidence that might prove someone sought an abortion despite knowing they were "too far along" in their pregnancy. As the stories in this book show, technologies that provide more information can be punishing when they mean to be liberating. This paradox is the story of the home pregnancy test.

I write this afterword in July 2022, days after the Supreme Court decision for *Dobbs v. Jackson Women's Health Organization*, which has overturned *Roe v. Wade*.[1] Abortions will now be harder to access in more than half of American states as laws banning abortion or limiting its accessibility are being implemented. I don't know what the reproductive landscape will look like in the coming years, but I do know that the home pregnancy test will play a role in almost every unplanned pregnancy and in most planned pregnancies, for better or worse. As abortion and reproductive healthcare become harder to access in a clinical setting, we will find ourselves relying on home pregnancy testing more than ever.

ACKNOWLEDGEMENTS

I wrote the entirety of this book during the COVID-19 pandemic, and so I am especially grateful to everyone who made its writing possible during a time when writing often felt impossible. I am more aware than ever how much we depend on a community of caretakers, family members, friends, and colleagues when we undertake any new project—or really any endeavor. These acknowledgements will be especially long because I feel so much gratitude for the networks of people that have supported me these last two years.

I will forever think of this book as my pandemic project, both because its writing took place during the pandemic and—fingers crossed—perhaps its publication will correspond with the end of it. Back in March 2020, when I was barely thinking about this project, I had no idea that in just over a year people would be posting rapid antigen Covid tests on social media asking for advice about faint second lines or demonstrating how the second line darkens as the viral load replicates in bodies. The technology of these and pregnancy tests is much the same, as many people have noticed and even joked about on social media as Covid home tests became more prevalent in late 2021 and early 2022. The experience of taking a home pregnancy test became more familiar than ever.

I first proposed this project in January 2020, and I still remember talking to Sarah Blackwood, Lauren Klein, and Kyla Schuller about my proposal during our last in-person meeting. We didn't realize then that after almost ten years of regularly meeting as a writing group—when multiple children, illnesses, and even interstate moves didn't stop us—a pandemic finally would. Our writing group will always be the barometer against which I measure all other writing groups. Sarah, Lauren, and Kyla have taught me so much about writing, and this book wouldn't have existed without them.

Even after my proposal was accepted, like many people with young children, I didn't have the time or mental energy to write during a stressful time when full-time, in-person school wasn't available because of the pandemic and the threat of a serious illness was constantly looming. But it was Emily Rapp Black's wonderful writing class, and the group of women in that class—Charlotte Dekanter Chung, Nadia Hannan, Minda Honey, and Christie Thompson—who finally motivated me to start writing again. They read the earliest draft of the first chapter I wrote for this book, and their encouraging words stayed with me throughout the entire process.

I am also grateful to so many institutions and the people who work in them, who made my own work here possible.

I can't imagine the last two years without my children's wonderful teachers, who made these stressful and confusing times easier for my now first and fourth graders. Thank you, Mr. Gabriel, Ms. Shuster, Ms. Pavlakis, Ms. Donelan, Ms. Whittaker, Ms. Friedman, and Ms. Rubenstein. Thank you to summer camps and after school programs, to community services and resources like public libraries and playgrounds. You made our lives bearable during a difficult time.

Thank you to the librarians at Queens College, and particularly to everyone who makes the invaluable interlibrary loan system run. I recognize that enormous amounts of labor go into processing ILL requests, and I am so grateful this system exists. (Thank you to Kristin Hart who told me not to feel guilty about requesting article after article.) Finally, I am forever indebted to my favorite New York institution of all, the New York Public Library, and particularly its research branch, the Schwarzman Building, which made this project possible because of its enormous wealth of digital resources. I thought I couldn't write this book during a pandemic when archives were closed to me until I learned just how much the NYPL could offer online. Then later, when conditions in the city were safer, I was offered a space in the Allen Room to complete this project and could also access the library's resources in hard copy. Thank you especially to librarians Melanie Locay and Julie Golia for their help.

Meg Crane returned my phone call in June 2020 and offered to meet with me, and her generosity transformed this project. I can't thank her enough, not only for designing

the first home pregnancy test but also for being so open
to sharing her incredible story and letting me retell it in
these pages. Glenn Braunstein similarly responded to my
email immediately and offered to talk on the phone. He
patiently explained some of the scientific discoveries that
led to advancements in pregnancy testing and helped me
piece together how his research contributed to the test we
use today. Jesse Olszynko-Gryn, who knows more about
the history of pregnancy testing than anyone on this
planet, shared his research with me and helped me better
understand the nuances of pregnancy test histories. Our
countless conversations and email exchanges are reflected
on every page, and certainly made this book a thousand
times better. Jesse, all mistakes and misinterpretations here
are mine. Jesse also introduced me to the New Zealand
reproduction research project, and Tatjana Buklijas, Heather
Dron, Jenny Bangham, and Birgit Nemec generously agreed
to offer feedback on a chapter draft. Thank you to Heather
Latimer who invited me to share a chapter draft with her
Reproductive Technologies reading group at the University
of British Columbia, Okanagan. I am also indebted to
Nursing Clio, the amazing history of medicine and gender
blog that invited me to be a regular contributor. I first wrote
about the pregnancy test for *Nursing Clio*, and it was this
short piece that inspired this project. Thank you especially
to Laura Ansley, managing editor extraordinaire, and to
R.E. Fulton, Sarah Handley-Cousins, Lauren MacIvor
Thompson, Eileen Sperry, and Jacqueline Antonovich, who

are some of the best editors and copyeditors who have ever read my work.

I truly have the most wonderful colleagues at Queens College, and if anything, these last few years have emphasized to me how lucky I am to be supported by such kind-hearted, intellectually sharp, and thoughtful people. I worry I will forget someone, but I will start with the people who read parts of this manuscript—and then who volunteered to read more of the manuscript. Thank you to Vanessa Pérez Rosario who read the entire manuscript, and who gave me thoughtful feedback over lunch during some of the quietest days ever known in Klapper Hall. Steven Kruger read my chapter on hormones and shared his experience working in an immunology lab in the 1980s. His recollections about the shift from radioimmunoassays to ELISAs and the procedures for isolating antibodies were invaluable. I found it delightful that I was able to find answers to some of my more obscure scientific questions from a colleague in my own department. Kate Schnur also volunteered to read more of my project and shared her always insightful feedback. Miles Grier whose expansive knowledge of both African American literature and pop culture led me to Richard Wright's *Black Boy* and *Murphy Brown*. Thank you to Vanessa Pérez Rosario, Glenn Burger, Kate Schnur, Steven Kruger, Ala Alryyes, Duncan Faherty, Carrie Hintz, Briallen Hopper, Siân Silyn Roberts, Talia Schaffer, Roger Sedarat, Fred Gardaphe, Nicole Cooley, Megan Paslawski, and Cliff Mak who participated in a faculty seminar that gave me such helpful feedback on my first chapter. Thank you to Glenn Burger for both chairing our department through some of the most difficult times and for being a friend. Thank you Veronica Schanoes for introducing me to the short story about glassmen, abortions, and pregnancy tests discussed in the last chapter. And to all my wonderful colleagues not yet mentioned who invariably heard me talk about this project at some point or another: Jason Tougaw, Marco Navarro, Amy Wan, Annmarie Drury, Caroline Hong, Hillary Miller, Kim Smith, Chris Williams, Sue Goldhaber, Sara Alvarez, Norka Blackman-Richards, and Seo-Young Chu.

At Bloomsbury, thank you to Ian Bogost, Christopher Schaberg, and Haaris Naqvi for believing in this project and making space for it in their wonderful Object Lessons series. Thank you to Éabha Puirseil for your careful reading and catching my mistakes. Thank you to Rachel Moore for shepherding the manuscript toward publication, and thank you to Anahi Molina for meticulous and thoughtful copyediting and creating the index. Thank you to Nivethitha Tamilselvan for managing all the final stages.

Thank you to all my friends whose love and care has continually sustained me. In New York, spending time talking and laughing with Laura Michelle Davis and Tali Horowitz replenished me. Laura also applied her sharp editorial skills to my entire manuscript. Tali's phone calls were often my day's highlight. From California, Aman Gill gave me a mini lesson in immunology and how antibodies work in ELISA tests. (And taught me how to correctly pronounce ELISA.)

Michele Friedner and Mara Green, members of MKM, kept me grounded every day. I don't know how I would have survived a pandemic without you. In Jackson Heights, my walks, hikes, and playground chats with M.K. Babcock, Danielle Kaplan, Julianna Lee, Lilla Toke, Joanna Sondheim, Kristen Lombardi, Jenica Nasworthy, Tracey DeBenedictis, Melissa Rodnon, Christopher Schlottman, and Lily Saint provided community and commiseration. Michele, Mara, and Joanna also read chapters and provided invaluable advice and copy edits.

My family reminds me that I'm writing a book by regularly asking if I'm done writing the book. To my father, Eli Weingarten, my mother Ronit Segal, my stepmother Daphna Thal Weingarten, and my stepsisters Channie Amato and Koren Jozana. Thank you also to my wonderful and supportive in laws, the Frosts, in Canada. And to my partner Corey Frost, who was there for (almost) all of my pregnancy tests, and who is always there. Ansel and Silvan: I will always remember the pregnancy tests that resulted in your existence. And thank you to my sister, Shelly Weingarten Kalish, who first inspired me to write about pregnancy tests because we share all our reproductive trials with each other. To (all my) sisters forever—

NOTES

Introduction

1 Randi Hutter Epstein, *Aroused: The History of Hormones and How They Control Just About Everything* (W.W. Norton, 2018), 97-99.

Chapter 1

1 On June 9, 2021, I interviewed Margaret Crane, or Meg as she prefers to be called, in her apartment. Her story in this chapter is from that conversation, and from a follow-up conversation we had over the phone on July 22, 2021.

2 In 2015, Crane sold the prototype to the Smithsonian Museum at auction, and it can now be viewed in their galleries. See Roger Catlin, "The Unknown Designer of the First Home Pregnancy Test Is Finally Getting Her Due," *Smithsonian Magazine*, September 21, 2015. <https://www.smithsonianmag.com/smithsonian-institution/unknown-designer-first-home-pregnancy-test-getting-her-due-180956684/>.

3 United Press International, "A do-it-yourself pregnancy test bared," *The Province* (Vancouver, BC), Oct. 12, 1977, p. 2.

4 David Zinman, "U.S. Opposing Sales of Pregnancy Test," *Newsday* (Suffolk Edition), May 18, 1971, p.11, and Cathy Yarbrough, "Pregnancy Checks are 50 Pct. Accurate," *The Atlanta Constitution* (Atlanta, GA), July 14, 1972, p. 34.

5 Betty Palik, "New home pregnancy test could be a Canadian export," *The Gazette* (Montreal, QC), Dec. 18, 1970, p. 22.

6 "Do-it-yourself pregnancy test," *The Province* (Vancouver, BC), Jan. 4 1971, p. 8.

7 Ruth Winter, "You can be your own physician in do-it-yourself-kit boom," *Calgary Herald* (Calgary, Alberta), Nov. 22, 1971, p. 33.

8 Cindy Skalsky, "Pregnancy Tests are Selling Slowly," *Detroit Free Press*, March 9, 1971, p. 21. The article opens with a woman admitting to a customs officer that the purpose of her trip was to buy a home pregnancy test. Rather than confiscate it—because they were not approved for sale in the US—he asked about its cost and reliability.

9 Off Our Backs, "You don't need a rabbit to know which way: Do it yourself pregnancy test," *Liberation News Service,* November 10, 1971, p. 6.

10 "Pharmacy Offers Test Service for Pregnancy, May be Illegal," *Asbury Park Press* (Asbury Park, NJ), April 15, 1973, p. 27.

11 "Pregnancy Test is Disputed, " *New York Times,* April 29, 1973, p. 80.

12 This prompted the *American Journal of Public Health* to solicit medical and legal reviews of Ova II, and they found that it was only accurate fifty percent of the time. Lawrence D. Baker, et al., "Evaluation of a 'Do-It-Yourself Pregnancy Test," *American Journal of Public Health* 66.2 (Feb. 1976), p. 166-167; Anita Johnson, "Do-it-yourself pregnancy testing," *American Journal of Public Health* 66.2 (Feb. 1976), p. 129- 131.

13 For more of this history see Joan H. Robinson, "Bringing the pregnancy test home from the hospital," *Social Studies of Science* 46.5 (2016), p. 649-674.

14 The Associated Press, "Pregnancy-test recall overruled," *The Record* (Hackensack, NJ), July 18, 1975, p. 2.

15 *United States v. Article of Drug*, United States District Court for the District of New Jersey, July 16, 1975, Civ. No. 745-72.

16 Jane E. Brody, "Personal Health," *New York Times*, Feb. 1, 1978, p. 11.

17 United Press International (UPI), "F.D.A. seeks appeal over pregnancy kit," *New York Times*, July 26, 1975, p. 13.

18 Dolores Katz, "Home pregnancy test," *The San Francisco Examiner,* Dec. 6, 1977, p. 25.

Chapter 2

1 "Pregnancy Test" (classified ad)," *Los Angeles Times,* Feb. 3, 1933, p. 28. The first classified ad for a pregnancy test appeared in a local Hollywood newspaper called *Los Angeles Evening Citizen News* on August 26, 1932 and advertised a pregnancy test that did not require a physical exam.

2 "A.Z. Pregnancy Test," *Los Angeles Times*, Dec. 16, 1934, p. 77.

3 Harry E. Kaplan, "The Aschheim-Zondek Hormone Test for Pregnancy," *California and Western Medicine* 31.6 (Dec. 1929), p. 412-413.

4 John J. Dorn, Jean R. Morse, and Edward I. Sugarman, "Early Pregnancy—A Hormone Test for its Diagnosis," *California and Western Medicine* 35.4 (Oct. 1931), p. 266- 269.

5 For more of this history, especially from a British perspective, see Jesse Olszynko-Gryn, "The demand for pregnancy testing: The Aschheim-Zondek reaction, diagnostic versatility, and laboratory services in 1930s Britain," *Studies in History and Philosophy of Biological and Biomedical Sciences* 47 (2014), p. 233–247.

6 Loomis, Frederic M. "Discussion on 'The Friedman Test for Pregnancy'" by Lyle G. McNeile and Philip A. Reynolds, *California and Western Medicine* 38.1 (January 1933), p. 1- 8.

7 For more about the history of abortion in California, see Alicia Gutierrez-Romine, *From the Back Alley to the Border: Criminal Abortion in California 1920-1969*, University of Nebraska Press, 2020.

8 Vichy water was likely just a reference to sparkling or carbonated water. Originally, Vichy water meant water from the naturally carbonated springs in Vichy, France.

9 Edward R. Elkan, "The Xenopus Pregnancy Test," *British Medical Journal* 17.2 (Dec. 1938), p. 1253-1274.

10 Ralph Clark, "Test on Frog Works," *Valley Times Today* (North Hollywood, CA), Sept. 14, 1961, p. 1.

11 Christopher W. Coates and Abner I. Weisman, "Pregnancy Test Frogs Being Bred at Will," *Journal of the American Medical Association* 124.7 (1944), p. 461.

12 Ken Davis, "South African Frog Gives Rapid Pregnancy Test," *Tampa Bay Times* (Tampa, FL), April 22, 1942, p. 14.

13 "25-Cent South African Frog is Perfect Test for Pregnancy," *Central New Jersey Home News* (New Brunswick, NJ), June 8, 1942, p. 3.

14 James T. Golden, Jr., "Frogs at Work in Testing Pregnancy; Covington Lab 98% Accurate," *Cincinnati Enquirer* (Cincinnati, OH), March 22, 1949, p.18; Roger W. Marsters, Marion E. Black, Jno. D. Randall, "An Evaluation of the Rana Pipiens Male Frog Pregnancy Test," *American Journal of Obstetrics and Gynecology* 60.4, p. 752-62. For more of this history see Jesse Olszynko-Gryn, "Pregnancy Testing with Frogs," *Reproduction: Antiquity to the Present*, Cambridge University Press, 2018, p. 672.

15 Rose L. Berman. "A Critical Evaluation of Biological Pregnancy Tests," *American Journals of Obstetrics and Gynecology* 72.2 (1956), p. 349-262. In 1940 Berman co-invented a pregnancy test using a rat to replace the rabbit.

16 Leif Wide and Carl Gemzell, "An Immunological Pregnancy Test," *Acta endocrinologica* 35 (1960), p. 261-267.

17 Judith Vaitukaitis's contribution to the science of the modern pregnancy test is described on the NIH's website, compiled by Sarah Leavitt here: <https://history.nih.gov/display/history/Pregnancy+Test+-+A+Thin+Blue+Line+The+History+of+the+Pregnancy+Test>. Direct quotations from Vaitukaitis and personal anecdotes are from a 2003 interview by Leavitt, which can be found on the NIH website here: https://history.nih.gov/display/history/Vaitukaitis%2C+Judith+L.+2003. See also Sarah Leavitt's essay about the home pregnancy test's history:

Sarah Leavitt, "'A Private Little Revolution': The Home Pregnancy Test in American Culture," *Bulletin of the History of Medicine* 80. 2, Summer 2006, p. 317-345.

18 Judith Vaitukaitis, Glenn D. Braunstein, Griff T. Ross, "A radioimmunoassay which specifically measures human chorionic gonadotropin in the presence of human luteinizing hormone," *American Journal of Obstetrics and Gynecology* 113.6 (July 1972), p. 751-758.

19 Vaitukaitis' radioimmunoassay for pregnancy testing used blood for its final results, and today, doctors, especially in fertility clinics, still conduct blood tests for pregnancy diagnosis. Whether urine or blood is used, however, all tests continue to detect beta-hCG as the means to diagnose pregnancy.

20 "A Pregnancy Test Hailed at Parley," *New York Times,* Dec. 20, 1973, p. 25.

Chapter 3

1 Renate Wittem-Sterzel, "Diagnosis: the doctor and the urine glass," *The Lancet* 354, Dec. 1999, p. 13.

2 Glenn D. Braunstein, "The Long Gestation of the Modern Home Pregnancy Test," *Clinical Chemistry* 60.1, Jan. 2014, p. 18-21.

3 Paul Ghalioungui, S.H. Khalil, Ahmed Ammar, "On an Ancient Egyptian Method of Diagnosing Pregnancy and Determining Foetal Sex," *Medical History* 7.3, 1963, p. 241-246.

4 The tests described in this paragraph are from Earle Henriksen, "Pregnancy Tests of the Past and Present,"

Western Journal of Surgical Obstetric Gynecology 85, 1941, p. 610-618.

5   Liselotte Adler-Kastner, "From *personae non gratae* in Vienna 1938 to respected citizens of Edinburgh: a vignette of my parents, Dr. Ernest Adler and Dr. Regina Kapeller-Adler," *Wien Klin Wochenschr: The Middle European Journal of Medicine* 110.4-5 (1998), p. 174-180; thank you to Jesse Olszynko-Gryn for introducing me to Kapeller-Adler's work.

6   Ann Oakley, *The Captured Womb: A History of the Medical Care of Pregnant Women,* New York: Basil Blackwell, 1984, p. 17.

7   Ibid., p. 20.

8   Lara Freidenfelds, *The Myth of the Perfect Pregnancy: A History of Miscarriage in America,* Oxford UP, 2020, p. 169; Samuel Hansen, "Bedside Medicine for Bedside Doctors," *California and Western Medicine* 39.5 (Nov. 1933), p. 335- 339.

9   Associated Press, "New Method Detects Stork," *Los Angeles Times*, March 14, 1941, p. 13; William S. Barton, "Quick Results Claimed in New Pregnancy Test," *Los Angeles Times,* June 5, 1950, p. 44.

10 Frederick Falls, Vincent Freda, Harold Cohen, "A Skin Test for the Diagnosis of Pregnancy," *American Journal of Obstetrics and Gynecology,* March 1941, p. 431-438.

11 At least one clinical trial of the Q-test found it to be unreliable. This 1945 study tested both the Q-test and Kapeller-Adler's histidine test and found neither to be sufficient: Squadron Officer J.F. Davey and Fight Officer

D.E. Daley, "A Critical Survey of Two Diagnostic Pregnancy Tests," *Canadian Medical Association Journal* 52 (April 1945) p. 371-376. The authors undertook this study because they were looking for a reliable pregnancy test that didn't use a live animal. They wanted to test women who had been recruited into military service for World War II.

12 Martin Gumpert, "News about Medicine," *Redbook* 92.5 (March 1949), p. 47.

13 Leo F. Godley, "Therapeutic Trends," *The Bulletin of the American Society of Hospital Pharmacists* 9.6, Dec. 1952, p. 614-615.

14 "Tablets Show if Pregnant," Press-Telegram (Long Beach, CA), Nov. 27, 1958, p. 21.

15 Cynthia Carroll, "Woman is Her Own Guinea Pig in More Accurate Pregnancy Test," *The Mobile Journal* (Mobile, AL), Dec. 22 1961, p. 5.

16 *Washington Post*, "Hormonal Pregnancy Test Dangerous to Unborn," *The Post-Standard* (Syracuse, NY), May 10, 1977, p. 1.

17 K.M. Laurence, "Risks and Benefits of the Use of Hormonal Pregnancy Test Tablets," *Nature* 240, Nov. 24, 1972, p. 241-242.

18 Jesse Olszynko-Gryn, "Risky hormones, birth defects and the business of pregnancy testing, Part I" *Perceptions of Pregnancy* Nov. 22, 2016 <https://perceptionsofpregnancy.com/2016/11/22/risky-hormones-birth-defects-and-the-business-of-pregnancy-testing-pt-i/> and "Part 2," Dec. 12, 2016 <https://perceptionsofpregnancy.com/2016/12/12/risky-hormones-birth-defects-and-the-business-of-pregnancy-testing-part-ii/ >.

19 Laurence, "Risks and Benefits."

Chapter 4

1 For another argument that complicates the narrative of the home pregnancy test's place in the sexual revolution, see Linda L. Layne's "The Home Pregnancy Test: A Feminist Technology?" *Women's Studies Quarterly* 37.1/2 (Spring—Summer, 2009), p. 61-79.

2 "Am I Really, Truly Pregnant?" *Parents* 55.6, June 1980, p. 8; Paula Adams Hillard, "Pregnancy Tests," *Parents* 57.6, June 1982, p. 82.

3 Midge Lasky Schildkraut, "New! A While-you-wait pregnancy test," *Good Housekeeping* 184.1, Jan. 1977, p. 160.

4 "It's a Baby, Maybe," *Changing Times* Nov. 1987, p. 138.

5 Margot Raven, "In-home test kits - solid new territory for drugstores," *Drug Topics* 129, Jan. 7, 1985.

6 Carol Ann Holcomb, "Home Pregnancy Test Kits: How Readable Are the Instructions?" Unpublished talk, 1982. Accessed through ERIC Educational Resources Information Center; Barbara G. Valanis and Carol S. Perlman, "Home Pregnancy Test Kits: Prevalence of Use, False Negative Rates, and Compliance with Instructions," *American Journal of Public Health* 72, 1982, p. 1034-1036.

7 Laura Beil, "Doctors give thumbs up to new, improved home pregnancy tests," *The Shreveport Journal* (Shreveport, Louisiana), Jan. 20, 1989, p. 25.

8 Shirley Kesselman, "To Your Health: In-home Pregnancy Tests," *Seventeen* 40.1, Jan. 1981, p. 61.

9 Brigitte Jordan, "Part One: The Self-Diagnosis of Early Pregnancy: An Investigation in Lay Competence," *Medical Anthropology* 1.2, Spring 1977, p. 1-38.

10 Andrea Tone, "Medicalizing Reproduction: The Pill and Home Pregnancy Tests," *Journal of Sex Research* 49.4, 2012, p. 319-327.

11 Jean Todd Freeman, "My Baby was Born in Prison," *Ladies' Home Journal* 96.7, Jul. 1979, p. 31.

12 "New Pregnancy Test Cuts Out the Chemistry Lesson," *New Scientist,* Jul. 21, 1988, p. 39.

13 Cara Appelbaum, "Carter-Wallace buys a new strategy for pregnancy tests," *Adweek's Marketing Week* 31.22, May 28, 1990, p. 10.

14 The story made the front page of the *New York Times:* Michael Wines, "Views on Single Motherhood are Multiple at White House," *New York Times*, May 21, 1992, p. 1.

15 Yvette C. Terrie, "Home Diagnostic Kits: Take One Test and Call the Doctor in the Morning," *Pharmacy Times,* Sept. 4, 2004. <https://www.pharmacytimes.com/view/2004-09-4520>.

16 Kelsey Tyssowski, "Pee is for Pregnant: The history and science of urine-based pregnancy tests," *Science in the News* (Harvard University Graduate School of Arts & Sciences), August 31, 2018,

<https://sitn.hms.harvard.edu/flash/2018/pee-pregnant-history-science-urine-based-pregnancy-tests/>.

17 Gynuity is currently working on making the test more widely available to health clinics in several developing countries. For information on how the test works visit: <https://gynuity.org/resources/how-to-use-multi-level-pregnancy-tests>. Thank you to Margaret MacDonald for telling me about this test.

18 Grace Dean, "This is the UK's first pregnancy test specifically for visually impaired women. Users feel their results, rather than seeing them," *Business Insider,* Nov. 14, 2020. <https://www.businessinsider.com/rnib-uk-accessible-pregnancy-test-for-blind-visually-impaired-women-2020-10>.

Chapter 5

1   Henry B. Safford, "Tell Me Doctor," *Ladies' Home Journal*, Dec. 1950, p. 31.

2   Goodrich Schauffler, "Tell Me Doctor," *Ladies' Home Journal*, April 1961, p. 13, 137-8.

3   Merrill Joan Gerber, "The Stork is a Wonderful Bird," *Redbook*, Feb. 1967, p. 84-85, 151-153.

4   Arthur Gordon, "The Last Straw," Redbook, May 1949, p. 38.

5   Alma Birk, "Mother 'M' is Not Always for Monster," *Cosmopolitan* 166.2, Feb. 1969, p. 70-73, 127.

6   Radovsky, Vicki Jo, "Talking with Susan Dey: 'I'm Trying To Save Women's Lives,'" *Redbook* 174.1, Nov. 1989, p. 18, 20, 22.

7   Richard Wright, *Black Boy*, Harper Collins [1945], 1998, p. 310- 314.

8   Janet E. Childerhose and Margaret MacDonald analyze the home pregnancy test as an example of a health tool that has been "domesticated." See "Health consumption as work: The home pregnancy test as a domesticated health tool," *Social Science & Medicine* 86 (2013): p. 1-8.

Chapter 6

1   "Clearblue Easy ad," 1997, https://www.youtube.com/watch?v=IGoFXThEvNc.

2   A.J. Jacobs, "David Lynch's Commercial Break," *Entertainment Weekly*, July 18, 1997. <https://ew.com/article/1997/07/18

/david-lynchs-commercial-break/>; Tamar Charry, "The offbeat film maker David Lynch directs a campaign for Unilever's home pregnancy test," *New York Times*, June 26, 1997, Sec. D, p. 6.

3 "E.p.t. home pregnancy test commercial," 1988, <https://www.youtube.com/watch?v=XUFFYmDdkGc>.

4 "E.p.t. home pregnancy test commercial," 1990, <https://www.youtube.com/watch?v=8EDqJa0f3Tg>.

5 "E.p.t. plus home pregnancy test commercial," 1986, <//www.youtube.com/watch?v=NEYspePNgQ8>.

6 "First Response, One Step Pregnancy Test Commercial," 1992. <https://www.youtube.com/watch?v=_q7Vpg9atlo&list=PLEqf8pU7tcmZGJFdgXODX4pmCRma5PvGg&index=5>; "e.p.t. plus home pregnancy test commercial," 1991. <https://www.youtube.com/watch?v=X4hd5nZodaU&list=PLEqf8pU7tcmZGJFdgXODX4pmCRma5PvGg&index=5>; and "e.p.t. plus home pregnancy test commercial," 1995. <https://www.youtube.com/watch?v=hN43HiSTUXA>.

7 "E.p.t. plus home pregnancy test commercial," 1994. <https://www.youtube.com/watch?v=M48vx018_fw>.

8 "E.p.t. plus home pregnancy test commercial," 1994. <https://www.youtube.com/watch?v=R0vO_122Oyw>.

9 "What does a positive pregnancy test really look like??" Forum on *The Bump,* Jan. 2015 (last edited Dec. 2019), <https://forums.thebump.com/discussion/12219554/what-does-a-positive-pregnancy-test-really-look-like>. Replies and views statistics were noted on July 16, 2021.

10 Atif Zeadna, et al., "A comparison of biochemical pregnancy rates between women who underwent IVF and fertile controls who conceived spontaneously," *Human Reproduction* 30.4,

2015, p. 783–788. Many popular websites about miscarriage cite even higher statistics, claiming that up to 75% of pregnancies end as chemical pregnancies. Given that many people would have no idea that they've had a chemical pregnancy, if they hadn't used a pregnancy test, it's difficult to get accurate numbers.

11 Lara Freidenfelds documents how the home pregnancy test, among other devices and cultural changes, has transformed our understanding of what a pregnancy is and what it means to miscarry. See Lara Freidenfelds, *The Myth of the Perfect Pregnancy: A History of Miscarriage in America,* Oxford University Press, 2020, p. 166-186.

12 Sonja Haller, "Do dollar store pregnancy tests actually work?" *USA Today*, Feb. 22, 2019. <https://www.usatoday.com/story/life/allthemoms/2019/02/22/are-dollar-store-pregnancy-tests-accurate/2939242002/>.

Chapter 7

1 Lizzy Rosenberg, "Can the Pregnancy Test Filter on TikTok determine your future?" *Distractify*, June 26, 2020, <https://www.distractify.com/p/pregnancy-test-filter-tiktok>.

2 Valerie Williams, "Posting A Positive Pregnancy Test On Social Media Is Gross, #SorryNotSorry," *Mommyish*, Jan. 5, 2015, <https://mommyish.com/dont-post-a-positive-pregnancy-test-on-facebook/>.

3 Janet Manley, "Celebrity Pregnancy is Big Business," *New York Times*, Jan. 23, 2021. <https://www.nytimes.com/2021/01/23/style/celebrity-pregnancy-social-media.html>.

4 Emily Rapp Black, *Sanctuary*, Random House, 2021.

5 "Moments in Love, Chapter One," *Master of None*, season 3, episode 1, dir. Aziz Ansari, Netflix, 2021.

Chapter 8

1 Alaya Dawn Johnson, "They Shall Inherit the Earth with Seeds of Glass," *Uncanny: A Magazine of Science Fiction and Fantasy*, 2013. <https://uncannymagazine.com/article/they-shall-salt-the-earth-with-seeds-of-glass/>. Originally published in *Asimov's Science Fiction*, January 2013.

2 Atwood, Margaret, *The Handmaid's Tale*, Random House, [1986] 1998, p. 305. Professor Pieixoto calls Romania "Rumania" in the novel, but he appears to be describing the real-life policies of the country.

3 Tammy Sullivan, "Challenging the New York National Guard's Discriminatory Pregnancy Testing Policy," *ACLU Speak Freely*, March 6, 2009. <https://www.aclu.org/blog/smart-justice/mass-incarceration/challenging-new-york-national-guards-discriminatory-pregnancy>.

4 Robert Dvorchak, "Babies Born to the Homeless Consigned to a Bleak Life," *Los Angeles Times*, Jul 31, 1988, p. 2.

5 Susie Cagle, "Why are Alameda County Jails Forcing Women to Take Pregnancy Tests?," *Prison Legal News*, Jan. 2016, p. 32.

6 Leni Zumas, *Red Clocks*, Little, Brown, and Co., 2018.

7 "No Guarantees: Sex Discrimination in Mexico's Maquiladora Sector," *Mexico* 8.6, US Department of Justice, Aug. 1996. <https://www.justice.gov/sites/default/files/eoir/legacy/2013/06/14/mexico_0896.pdf>.

8 "Triple Discrimination: Woman, Pregnant, and Migrant," *Fair Labor Association,* March 2018. <https://www.fairlabor.org/sites/default/files/documents/reports/triple_discrimination_woman_pregnant_and_migrant_march_2018.pdf>.

9 United Press International, "Firm Gives Applicants Secret Pregnancy Test" *Philadelphia Daily News* (Philadelphia, PA), Jul. 18 1970, p.11.

10 Associated Press, "Report: Secret Pregnancy Test for Police," *Philadelphia Daily News* (Philadelphia, PA), Nov. 5, 1987, p. 27.

11 Adam Shaw, "Nielsen: ICE giving pregnancy tests to migrant girls as young as 10 after dangerous journey to border," *Fox News*, Mar. 6, 2019. <https://www.foxnews.com/politics/nielsen-ice-gives-pregnancy-tests-to-migrant-girls-as-young-as-10-after-dangerous-journey-to-border>.

12 Brit Bennett, *The Mothers,* Riverhead Books, 2016, p. 11.

13 Katrina Kimport, "Pregnant Women's Reasons for and Experiences of Visiting Antiabortion Pregnancy Resource Centers," *Perspectives on Sexual and Reproductive Health* 52.1, Mar. 2020, p. 49-56.

14 Amy G. Bryant and Jonas J. Swartz, "Why Crisis Pregnancy Centers Are Legal but Unethical," *AMA Journal of Ethics,* Mar. 2018.<https://journalofethics.ama-assn.org/article/why-crisis-pregnancy-centers-are-legal-unethical/2018-03>; "She said abortion could cause breast cancer: A Report on: The Lies, Manipulations, and Privacy Violations of Crisis Pregnancy Centers in New York City," NARAL and National Institute for Reproductive Health, Oct. 2010. <https://www.nirhealth.org/wp-content/uploads/2015/09/cpcreport2010.pdf>.

15 Khiara M. Bridges, *Reproducing Race: An Ethnography of Pregnancy as a Site of Racialization,* University of California Press, 2011, p. 34.

16 Ling Ma, *Severance,* Farrar, Straus, and Giroux, 2018.

17 Louise Erdrich, *Future Home of the Living God,* Harper Perennial. 2017, p. 3.

18 *False Positive*, directed by John Lee (Hulu, 2021).

19 Dorothy Roberts, *Killing the Black Body: Race, Reproduction, and the Meaning of Liberty*, Vintage, 1998.

Afterword

1 See *Dobbs v. Jackson Women's Health Organization*, <https://www.supremecourt.gov/opinions/21pdf/19-1392_6j37.pdf>.

INDEX